Addressing

Domestic Violence

in the Workplace

JOHNNY LEE

Dear Myron,

Thank you so much

It was great meeting you.

HRD PRESS, Inc.
Amherst, Massachusetts

Published by:
HRD Press
22 Amherst Road
Amherst, MA 01002-9709
800-822-2801 (U.S. and Canada)
413-253-3488
413-253-3490 (Fax)
www.hrdpress.com

ISBN 0-87425-838-3

Editorial services by Suzanne Bay and Sally Farnham
Typeset by Wordstop, Madras, India
Cover design by Eileen Klockars
Printed in Canada

Acknowledgments

I would like to express my appreciation for the support and encouragement to the following individuals and programs:

Dr. Lenore Walker

The Domestic Violence Intervention Project

Kim Wells and the Corporate Alliance to End Partner Violence

Debra Collins and the DAC House

The North Carolina Coalition against Domestic Violence

Ann Kaminstein of DV Initiative, Inc.

Barbara Marlowe

Coleen Gorski

Rita Starliper

Dr. David Compton

Dr. Carol Runyan and The Injury Prevention Research Center in Chapel Hill, NC

Donna Norton and the Family Violence Prevention Fund

Dr. Beverly Urban

And most importantly, my family

This is dedicated to all the victims of abuse who had the courage to leave the violence and make a better life for themselves and their children.

Contents

Preface

The goal of this book is to help victims of abuse find support and protection at their workplace. Some decision-makers will pick up this book to learn how to prevent a shooting that would disrupt productivity and cause turmoil in the workplace, and learn that the problem of domestic violence is far more complex and insidious. The chapters that follow will clearly demonstrate why it is in every company's best interest to help those employees who are victims of domestic violence or who are responsible for it in their own lives. A workplace that implements measures, trains its staff, and helps its employees will be safer and more productive.

Human resource professionals, managers, and business owners will find the information useful in developing an effective response to the increasing threat of domestic violence in the workplace. Whether it is to prevent an incident through policy and program development or to be ready to intervene in a crisis, I hope the information helps organizations and employers support their employees and prevent a tragedy. Domestic violence advocates, employment law attorneys, security personnel, and occupational health professionals will find the material indispensible as they inform the business community about this serious problem.

Every attempt was made to cover all the issues related to domestic violence in the workplace, but there is much more to learn about this important subject. By becoming involved with local efforts and the numerous national programs described herein, an organization can quickly find the support and validation it will need to address and prevent this terrible crime that so pervades our modern society.

References and descriptions of actual incidents of workplace violence appear throughout the book. I have done my best to protect the anonymity of the victims, but I recognize that I did not seek their permission to describe their experiences. I only hope they will understand that my writing about real and actual occurrences will help convince the intended audience of the book to do whatever they can to support and protect victim employees. It is critical to their safety and survival.

Thank you for being concerned enough to read this book. I hope that it results in one more victim becoming a survivor rather than a fatality because their employer and co-workers took steps to protect their employees at work.

A portion of the proceeds from the sale of
Addressing Domestic Violence in the Workplace
will go toward the work of Helpmate, Inc.,
a domestic-violence shelter in Asheville,
North Carolina.

Chapter 1

Recognizing the Warning Signs

Joseph Ferguson was a supervisor working for a security firm in California in 2001 when his co-worker–girlfriend told him that she wanted to break up with him. Ferguson reacted by taking an axe to the woman's car, which was parked in the company parking lot. He was put on immediate suspension while the company assessed the risk he posed to the other employees. Ferguson had a favorable work history and a clean criminal record, but co-workers reported that he was a bit eccentric in habit and beliefs. In fact, he was considered a fanatic militant who had extreme right-wing beliefs and a shooting range in his basement.

The company began to recognize the severity of the threat, and took steps to deal with it, but before a plan to deal with the threat was implemented, tragedy struck: Ferguson returned to his job with an arsenal of weapons two days after being suspended, fatally shot his ex-girlfriend and another worker. He then left the work site and drove to a client company's facility, where he gunned down another man in apparent retribution for recently having to cover that guard's shift. A second employee of that client company, in the wrong place at the wrong time, was also killed. Another security guard at yet another location was more fortunate: Ferguson handcuffed her to a tree and left her there while he took off with her radio and vehicle for the home of someone else he was angry with. The man and his wife were taken hostage and terrorized throughout the night. He videotaped himself and eventually killed the man, but in the morning set the man's wife free with the videotape. She immediately contacted authorities, who located Ferguson and promptly surrounded him with an emergency response team. Thus began a long and deadly shootout: Armed with a fully automatic AK-47, a sawed-off shotgun, and a bulletproof vest, Ferguson fired away, critically wounding an innocent bystander when a hollow-point round went through the man's car door and hit him. Ferguson eventually committed suicide, ending a bloody rampage that began with a romantic rejection.

What a terrible tragedy. Could something like this take place at your facility?

"There are no victims of domestic violence in my workforce. I see all of my employees every day, and none of them look like they are getting hit."

You will learn more than you ever knew about domestic abuse from this book. What's more, you will understand how close the threat is to your employees and your company's productivity, and what you can do to prevent or minimize its impact. We will start by explaining the less-than-obvious warning signs of domestic abuse—the emotional, psychological, and behavioral aspects that need to be considered along with the physical indications.

Let's start with a working definition of **domestic violence:**

> *Domestic violence* is a pattern of behavior meant to intimidate and control the victim. The harassment, persecution, and physical abuse cause the victim to suffer psychologically, socially, and emotionally. The abuse can come in the form of physical, sexual, emotional, and/or mental trauma, but often the mere threat of violence allows the abuser to maintain manipulative control over the victim.

A black eye or a swollen lip is a good indication that an employee is being victimized, but in many cases the abuse will not be so apparent.

The terms *domestic abuse* and *domestic violence* each refer to physical assaults or patterns of behaviors meant to intimidate, control, and manipulate. In many situations, a single violent episode is all that is needed to strike fear into the heart of the victim. From then on, the abuser only needs to raise his or her voice or fist to suggest that the nightmare will reoccur.

It is vitally important that every employee, particularly supervisors, HR staff members, and co-workers, become familiar with the signs of abuse, because they are likely to step in first; an employee rarely comes to management with their fears. Victims are reluctant to identify themselves as such, and might not even consider themselves as victims of domestic violence. In fact, there is a strong tendency for victims to minimize or deny the reality of their situation—not because they are weak or lack intelligence, but because it helps them endure the hardships. Denial serves as a self-defense mechanism. The employer's role play in such circumstances is vital.

Victims of domestic violence feel a tremendous amount of shame and embarrassment about their role in the relationship, and are extremely reluctant to disclose. Their self-esteem and ego are already being destroyed by the abuser—the last thing they want is for people to pity them and wonder why they take the abuse. To be identified as a victim further lowers self-worth.

Why is it so difficult? As a society, we are judged, rightly or wrongly, by the success of our relationships, just as much as our material possessions and occupational status. Victims go to great lengths to present themselves in happy relationships; they try desperately to keep their family and personal well-being stable and secure, and they do this by putting on a happy face and becoming the picture of contentment. If they are recognized as a victim of abuse, they feel as if they have failed to maintain this image. This is why it is so important to be supportive and understanding when you speak to the victim about their personal crisis, and why it is all the more important that co-workers and supervisors identify and address the problem before it becomes a job performance or even a safety concern.

What are the less-than-obvious signs of abuse? Can employers, managers, supervisors, and co-workers tell from the way a person looks or acts that an individual is being abused by a current or former intimate partner?

Physical Indications

Physical signs of domestic violence include noticeable marks such as bruises, scratches, and handprints from violent grabs (supposedly due to clumsiness or an accident). The victim, anxious to hide the marks, will sometimes come to work wearing a turtleneck or a long-sleeve top to hide the handprints on their arms and wrists, or wear long pants in warm weather to hide kick marks on their calves. Some women put on a great deal of makeup in an attempt to cover or redirect attention from facial injuries. Dark sunglasses worn inside can hide swollen or black eyes, or eyes that are bloodshot from hours of crying or sleep deprivation. Inappropriate or odd dress habits can also be a sign that the person is hiding signs of physical abuse.

Sometimes the marks from an attack are in areas where they are not readily observable. Batterers strike blows to the stomach and chest, on the upper legs, or on the head behind the hairline so acquaintances and the police won't easily see the injury. This deliberate craftiness makes it obvious that domestic violence is not a simple moment of rage and loss of control: **Abusers know where to strike their victims to inflict pain and not leave any evidence.** Look for any of the following apparent physical signs that the individual is in pain or hurting:

▲ Visible injuries or signs of trauma, such as bruises or scars
▲ Bruises or handprints on wrists or throat
▲ Signs of hair being pulled out
▲ Excessive makeup

▲ Clothing or accessories that might be worn to cover injured areas
▲ Limping or tenderness in joints or muscles
▲ Moving slowly or carefully because of pain or soreness

Behavioral Indications

Clearly, a woman or man who is being battered will not act chipper or bubbly. Degradation and abuse wear down a person's self-esteem to the point where they become withdrawn and depressed. They feel hostility, guilt, shyness, anger, and a whole range of contradictory emotions that tend to confuse friends and co-workers. Their feelings of hopelessness and sadness will cause them to withdraw from people at work, perhaps holing-up in their office space or workstation out of embarrassment by their physical injuries. Many experience a very real need to be near their phone in case the abuser calls—sometimes their abuser requires this.

A battered employee is often reluctant to get involved in social or group activities and is unlikely to attend office parties around the holidays or other gatherings. Going out to lunch with others clearly violates the abuser's wish to isolate the victim. (These are hardly decisive signs of an abused person, but they are pieces in the puzzle.) Look for signs that the victim feels compelled to return straight home after work: An extra five minutes on their trip home or even an extra mile on the odometer in the car is likely to be met with suspicion and accusations, as would socializing with co-workers.

Abusers have other ways of maintaining control, such as limiting the victim's financial resources. The abused employee might never have any money for themselves to buy new clothes or personal items, or to go out to lunch with friends or co-workers. These are "luxuries" they cannot afford. Anything having to do with their paycheck is likely to be strictly supervised and controlled; many abusers, in fact, regularly check to see if the victim is hiding money.

Perhaps the most evident behavioral sign of abuse is obvious fear. If the two are together, the victim might be silent or defer all questions and comments to him or her. If the victim is alone, sudden noises or movements will probably startle them. Hyper-vigilance is also a common indication of post-traumatic stress disorder, which victims of abuse experience in their world of constant trauma and threat. If the victim has already found the courage to leave the abuser, this fear can turn into outright terror that the abuser will call or try to see them at work. Be alert for this fear (and how strong it is), because it can be an indication that violence is imminent.

Look for signs of any of these emotions:

▲ Depression   ▲ Anger
▲ Guilt   ▲ Sadness
▲ Fear   ▲ Irritability
▲ Anxiety   ▲ Fatigue
▲ Withdrawal   ▲ Desperation

Job Productivity and Performance

Physical and behavioral indications rarely capture the whole picture of a battered or abused employee. A manager or supervisor might first notice problems with job performance. The most obvious indication is frequent tardiness, going home early, or missing entire days of work. This kind of behavior is a clear sign that something is amiss.

What is the employee going through? Simply this: The abuse she is experiencing at home has such a debilitating effect that she is not able to come to work on time (or even at all). The physical trauma might even be so bad that she can't do the work or even attempt to get dressed and leave the house. A large percentage of victims are women who at some point need urgent care or emergency medical assistance because of domestic violence: If the woman is not able to adequately hide her injuries, she might call in sick until the marks heal. When sick leave and vacation time run out, she'll just not show up or request time off without pay. If the company or organization has a staff nurse or an in-house health center, victims of abuse will probably use this health benefit more frequently.

Harassment also affects work productivity, because it takes a toll on the victim's health and opportunities to relax and de-stress. If a victim is kept up all night and is forced to endure verbal, sexual, and/or physical harassment or cruelty, she will struggle to stay awake and prepare for work. Housekeeping chores, children, grocery shopping, and hours of harassment and intimidation make it nearly impossible to get to work on time.

Many abusers attempt to sabotage the victim's arrangements concerning childcare and transportation. She'll have to leave work early if she gets a call saying he is too drunk to pick up the kids at school like he promised, or he "forgot." A partner's failure to support the victim's commitment to work is another subversive means of getting the victim fired and making her even more dependent on the abuser. Firing the victim-employee gives the abuser what he wants.

On a positive note, sometimes the reason why a victim misses work is because she is trying to leave the abuser. Court appearances and meetings with advocates, law enforcement officers, and attorneys take up a tremendous amount of time. If a victim feels that the employer will be sympathetic and supportive, she might explain why time off is needed.

What about their job performance? The first indication of a problem might be when the victim's work performance deteriorates. How can anyone operate at peak performance when they are forced to endure an entire night of lectures, humiliating abuse, or even demands to perform degrading sexual acts? It is impossible for a victim to forget about what happened the night before, so she will be anxious about what she will have to face upon arrival home. A victim might be an exemplary employee yet have periods of marked deficiencies (they tend to follow the cyclical nature of the abuse). When things are going well at home, the employee can function, but when there are periods of violence and threat, job productivity is affected because it is difficult to concentrate and focus on the tasks at hand. This is particularly dangerous if the nature of work requires one's full attention to maintain safety.

Look for these job performance problems that might be signs of abuse:

- ▲ Tardiness
- ▲ Leaving early
- ▲ Increased use of sick benefits (time off and medical expenses)
- ▲ Mistakes or forgetfulness
- ▲ Fear or reluctance to answer the phone
- ▲ Fear or anxiety about leaving the building or going to the parking lot
- ▲ Absenteeism
- ▲ Excessive time spent on the phone or on personal tasks

The Abuser's Behavior

Be alert to behavioral indications on the part of the partner. You can often tell when the couple has finally broken up: When a victim has left the abuser, the partner often resorts to stalking and harassing, but if they are still together and the victim is trying to keep the relationship free from violent episodes, there will probably be other signs. Consider the boyfriend that always stops by his partner's work: He brings flowers and candy, and hangs around during her lunch hour. He calls frequently throughout the day. Other co-workers express praise and envy that the employee has such an attentive romantic interest, but the truth is that he is keeping track of what he considers his "property."

When the relationship turns to the abusive phase or the victim attempts to end the relationship, contact can become more frequent and malignant. The number of phone calls increases, each becoming more offensive and threatening. The victim will appear visibly upset after such calls or messages. This common form of harassment might even raise the concerns of nearby co-workers.

Stalking seems to be the most unnerving behavior to the victim and the rest of the employees. The abuser tries to repeatedly visit the victim; if he or she is turned away, the abuser is likely to wait in the parking lot or across the street. This single-mindedness and no apparent need to go to work or behave appropriately is what truly scares anyone associated with the experience. Abusers usually know just how far they can push and are constantly testing the boundaries of what the employer will accept. This highly focused obsession and continuous harassment is a very critical warning sign of potential danger. Do not take it lightly.

Conclusion

It is important to understand that these behaviors do not actually signify that a relationship is abusive. They are warning signs, and we list them to provide supervisors, managers, and employees with things to look out for. When there is concern about a particular individual, any of these behaviors should be considered.

However, these descriptions provide only a glimpse into the relationship between victim and abuser. Training and awareness about domestic violence is extremely critical, and it is readily available through outreach programs. Consult the partial list of agencies listed in the appendix, but be sure to contact your local domestic-violence organization first. If you are not sure what you are seeing has to do with abuse, talk with an experienced counselor or advocate to determine the seriousness of the situation and identify next steps.

Unfortunately, in the most horrific and dangerous cases of domestic violence, there were few warning signs. There have been far too many accounts of friends and relatives of a homicide victim claiming that they had no idea that anything was wrong. The victim might have been very good at hiding the abuse, or the abuser was extremely clever in their control-seeking behavior that the most astute of observers failed to notice. Clearly, an accepting, understanding work environment is even more critical if the victim is to feel comfortable enough to come forward.

This is why leadership and supervisor skills are so important. A perceptive manager must be able to pick up on the warning signs that an employee needs help. Just how to make that approach and broach the issue or handle the discussion once it is disclosed requires the same amount of sensitivity and attention.

Chapter 2

The Costs and Impact of Domestic Violence on a Business Organization

The phone at the store rang all day long. Sometimes Karl Knapp would just hang up when someone answered, but if Jane J., his estranged girlfriend, took the call, he would demand to see her again. He had just gotten out of jail, and though she had had enough of the relationship, she agreed to drop the restraining order. Karl, however, refused to accept the fact that the relationship was over.

Tired of his constant barrage of calls, a worker at the Albuquerque window dressing shop allegedly spoke to him about the threats on January 3rd, 2003. Perhaps this person did not know that Jane's ex had a violent criminal history and was capable of inflicting more violence. When he arrived at the store at 4:00 p.m. and started threatening and harassing Jane, the store owner told him to leave immediately. This started the rampage: Karl Knapp shot and killed the owner. Then when Jane J. fled to the business next door, he followed her there and murdered the store manager as he tried to defend Jane. The courageous effort of both men to stop Knapp from taking revenge on his ex-girlfriend for filing three criminal charges against him and finally ending their two-year relationship was to no avail: He killed her as well. He then fled to a nearby pawn shop and barricaded himself in. After a three-hour standoff with the police, Knapp attempted to take his own life, but failed. He was the sole and least-worthy survivor of the rampage that, in one short afternoon, destroyed three businesses and (much more importantly) caused three families to suffer devastating loss.

A business owner's worst fear is workplace violence. Incidents such as the one described above are gratuitously reported by the media, analyzed by security professionals, and etched into the community's history for years to come. As violent and frightening as they are, however, they represent only a small percentage of the ways that domestic abuse threatens and impacts the organization. Many impacts are more subtle and thus more insidious, but they do not engender as much attention. This next situation is representative of what happens in stores, offices, and factories throughout the country. Chances are pretty good that you have or will have someone on your workforce who is being abused by a partner and going through a similar ordeal.

One of the company's employees has been increasingly arriving late for work or is calling in sick 30 minutes after the shift starts. Her sudden "illnesses" are not surprising, since she has filed more than the average number of health benefit claims. When she is at work, she can't seem to concentrate on the task, and makes frequent mistakes. Her supervisor decides to sit down with the woman to discuss these inconsistencies but does not get very far in the discussion, because the employee suddenly blurts out that she can't work anymore and will be leaving at the end of the day, without even a two-week notice. The supervisor had no intention of dismissing the woman, who was meeting or exceeding expectations before this recent slump. However, she was not inclined at this point to persuade the employee to stay. She does indeed quit her job that day, and no one gives any thought to what might be going on. Business as usual.

Of the Karl Knapp episode and the situation described above, which has a bigger impact on the company? The crisis from a violent rampage is unbelievably overwhelming because there is no way to measure the trauma inflicted on the victims and their families. But the second situation is so much more common: It takes place every day in businesses and organizations of every shape and size, so it has a much more detrimental and prolonged impact on the economy. While so much media attention is given to violent incidents, the reality is that domestic violence itself carries tremendous consequences on thousands of businesses *without a single shot having been fired.*

In this chapter, we outline the broad range of effects domestic violence has on businesses and organizations. The continuum begins with the deterioration of an employee's productivity due to abuse that generally takes place outside of work and extends to interruptions and harassment at work. If gone unchecked, it is likely to end only with a devastating tragedy that can literally close the doors of a business that is unprepared. The abuser must not be forgotten in this equation: his (or her) behavior often affects his work performance and creates a direct liability on the part of his own employer who perhaps should have seen it coming.

The Prevalence of Domestic Violence

It is hard not to be aware of a violent incident once it begins, but strangely enough, there are employers who do not believe that they should be concerned about domestic violence. After all, the very word *domestic* refers to personal affairs that take place in a home. Some employers naively assume that none of *their* employees have been or are currently victims of abuse. The reality is that domestic violence causes more trauma to women than automobile accidents, rape, and muggings *combined!* The overwhelming and growing prevalence of domestic violence in our communities makes it more than likely that there are or will soon be victims listed on your employee roster. There is no way to truly measure how many employees are experiencing family violence, but an in-depth study of two manufacturing plants in Illinois did produce some revelations: 29 percent of the women employees who responded reported that they had experienced physical abuse at some point in their lives; 16 percent had been violently attacked by a domestic partner just within the past year (Urban, et al., 1999). The study showed that men are also legitimate victims of abuse, deserving the same support and protection: 19 percent of the men who responded to this same survey said that they experienced abuse, and 10 percent reported that the abuse occurred within the past year. However, domestic violence is generally a woman's issue, as numerous, well-documented studies show. The great majority of research points to women as the predominant, frequent, and repeated targets of this heinous crime.

2002 Report of Violent Victimizations Perpetrated by an Intimate Partner

Gender of Victim	Number of Violent Assaults in the U.S.	Percentage of Total Assaults
Male	72,520	3%
Female	494,570	20%

Source: U.S. Department of Justice—Bureau of Justice Statistics

In a national survey, conducted in 1997, approximately 24 percent of women between the ages of 18 and 65 (the prime employment years) reported that they had experienced domestic violence at some point in their lives (U.S. Department of Justice, November, 2000). While **domestic violence** is defined broadly as **a pattern of behavior meant to control a victim,** statistics clearly show that physical violence is often used to maintain that control. A similar study found more-striking results: Almost one-third of American women (31 percent) reported being physically or sexually assaulted by an intimate partner at some point in their lives (Collins, et al., 1999). In 2001, the United States Bureau of Justice reported that more than 500,000 women in the United States reported that they have been the victim of non-fatal assaults by an intimate partner. The actual number of incidents that occurs is likely to be many times this figure, because an astounding number of domestic assaults are never reported.

Impact on Work Performance

The abuse that victims endure at home affects them in the workplace, impairing their ability to do their job. In one survey of survivors who were employed at the time of the abuse, 37 percent of the victims stated that it affected their job in a variety of ways, including being late for work, missing work altogether, or even causing them to eventually lose their job.

It is difficult to assess how the abuse affects a victim's inability to concentrate on their work. The threats, sexual assaults, and physical abuse can be devastating and harrowing no matter where the victim is. Imagine a long night having to plead for mercy, being forced to perform degrading acts, and repeatedly being assaulted. If the individual is able to come in to work the next day, surely she cannot be the optimal performer she was when she was first hired. The inability to take her mind off the abuse results in mistakes in calculation, difficulty working with peers or customers, and even compromises in workplace safety, depending on the employee's responsibilities. We all understand how personal issues can interfere with one's concentration at work, but the magnitude and turmoil that surrounds domestic abuse pushes an employee to the limits of their ability to cope.

Lack of concentration might be hard to quantify, but absenteeism isn't. In fact, it is a clear, objective indicator of how domestic violence reduces workforce production. When a victim calls in sick, she is doing so because she is ashamed of visible injuries or needs to seek medical attention. She won't be able to do even the minimal amount of work required. Tardiness or leaving early are also red flags that have a direct impact on a worker's ability to get the job done. In an often-quoted New York study, researchers found that 56 percent of the survivors surveyed responded that they were late for work at least five days in a one-month period, and 28 percent stated that they had to leave early at least the same number of days because of the abusive relationship. And over half of those surveyed (54 percent) stated that they were forced to miss at least three full days of work in an average month. This same study noted that over half of these survivors lost a job mainly due to the abuse (Couper, et al., 1987). A more recent study had even more disparaging results. Up to 85 percent of the victims surveyed missed work due to the abuse; again, just over half lost their jobs (Ahrens, et al., 2000).

Injury is not the only reason for tardiness or absence. Abusers often create problems in order to interfere with the victim's job or simply out of sheer spite. They fail to keep a promise to pick up the children from school, make demands at the last minute, or even take away a partner's transportation in order to force the victim to choose between physical retaliation or their job. In one survey of abuse survivors, 44 percent reported that the abuser hid the car keys or even disabled the car to prevent them from going to work. Another 20 percent said that the abusing partner took the money that was needed for public transportation or otherwise prevented them from leaving for work. Employers tend to grow tired of employees' excuses, yet victims rarely explain the real source of the disruption (Gist, et al., 2000). (In the next chapter, we will look at why abusers feel the need to endanger the victim's employment.)

In one study conducted at a manufacturing plant, the average absenteeism of an identified victim was 30 percent higher than the average worker. These workers were also 12 percent more likely to be disciplined for performance issues (Urban, 2000).

This combination of poor performance, tardiness, and absenteeism makes a prodigious economic impact on the organization. One study concluded that businesses lose an estimated $727.8 million annually, a large portion of which was attributed to the 7.9 million paid workdays lost due to the abuse (U.S. Dept. of Health and Human Services, March 2003). The knee-jerk solution to this problem is often dismissal or termination; the employer simply feels that the employee must be let go in order to find someone who *will* get the job done. However, this solution is never as easy as it sounds. Every Human Resources professional knows that the time, money, and effort it takes to advertise, review résumés, interview, hire, and train a new person is costly. It is much easier to address a current employee's problems than to bring in a fresh recruit.

However, employers are usually not the ones making the decision. Domestic violence often forces victims to quit, without the employer ever knowing why. A small retail shop once found itself losing sales for no apparent reason; one of its sales clerks (who sold more clothing than any other employee, even though she was only there part-time) suddenly announced that she was leaving. This was a woman who had never been late for work, always kept the store assiduously tidy, and never received a personal phone call at the store. The manager was understandably disappointed and perplexed at her decision to leave. They had a good working relationship, and it was obvious that the employee liked coming to work— and her performance reflected that enjoyment. The manager offered more pay and flexible scheduling to get her to stay, to no avail, never realizing that the employee's husband was jealous and told her to quit. No threats or violence were used to influence her decision—she just knew what would happen if she refused to quit.

Impact on Health Care Costs

Let us look at one more cost of which all employers are acutely aware: health care benefits. Abuse has a serious impact on the bottom line of any company, particularly in this area. Domestic violence has long been regarded as a serious and epidemic public health threat to women: The combined costs of emergency room visits, clinical appointments, pain medication, and mental health services is staggering, and it directly impacts employers who offer their employees medical insurance. The cost of health care, including medical attention and mental health support, by the Department of Health and Human Services published in 2003 is estimated to be almost $4.1 billion nationwide. One preliminary study demonstrates the cost to an individual plan much more succinctly: A victim of abuse will incur $1,755 more in medical expenses than the average woman employee—a 92 percent difference (Gilmer, et al., 1999). This figure might stun some employers, but business accountants are well aware of this. A survey in 1994 by Liz Claiborne noted that 44 percent of business executives recognized domestic violence as a major cause of the increases in health care expenses (Patrice Tanaka, 2002).

Continuing Abuse in the Workplace

Employers are usually not aware of the abuse when it follows the victim to work. More than 13,000 incidents of domestic abuse are committed every year at the workplace: harassment by phone or in person, stalking, damage to property, physical assault, and even murder (Zachary, 1998).

One discreet but common way to exert control over the victim is by calling or sending an e-mail. He or she can continue the abuse by contacting the victim at work, without ever having to come to the job site. If the two are still in the "relationship," the abuser is likely to contact the victim randomly out of the jealous fear that their partner might be having an affair. It is not uncommon for an abuser to pressure their partner to wear a pager or carry a cell phone and immediately respond or risk suspicious rage. The incessant calls are meant to intimidate, punish, or even coerce the victim to stay in the relationship. These constant calls can be extremely disruptive to co-workers and management, and in many, many cases they eventually result in the victim's dismissal, thereby pushing the victim back into the abusive relationship.

So how often does this occur? One U.S. congressional report estimated that 35 to 56 percent of employee-victims are harassed while they are at work (U.S. General Accounting Office, 1998). Another study of survivors of domestic violence found that abusive partners harassed 74 percent of their victims at their job—three quarters out of every four victims (Couper, 1987). These calls and constant messages not only interrupt concentration and production, but they are also very distressing to the victim. Cruel and virile threats can deliver a devastating blow to the victim's ability to pay full attention to their normal duties. An employee who is threatened in graphic detail with physical and sexual malice might not want to answer the phone at all.

Actual Violence

The violence in some domestic relationships will spill over into the workplace, and women employees are clearly at risk. An intensive review of North Carolina's occupational homicides for the years 1999, 1998, and 1997 revealed that it was an ex-husband or ex-boyfriend who caused 75 percent of all female fatalities (Morracco, 2000).

Nationally, homicide was the leading cause of death for women on the job until the year 2000, when it slipped into second place behind accidents. While the homicides by co-workers and business customers have generally declined in the past few years, the number of homicides committed by partners or ex-partners has remained the same and in some cases has actually risen.

Workplace Homicides in the United States

Where the perpetrator is a ...	Average 1994–1998	1998	1999	2000	2001
Co-worker (or ex-worker)	69	63	62	75	53
Customer/client	36	35	41	37	32
"Intimate partner" (husband, boyfriend, or former partner)	26	20	31	28	34

Source: Bureau of Labor Statistics, Department of Labor

The immediate expenses related to a shooting incident are easily calculated. Damaged equipment and property must be repaired or replaced. There will be separate costs related to trauma clean-up services, because custodial staffs are generally unwilling or incapable of handling the bio-hazardous material. There will also be costs related to lost production or sales during the crisis, as well as factory or store shutdowns so law enforcement personnel can gather evidence and document the crime scene, especially in complicated cases. Insurance might cover some or all of these expenditures, but this, in turn, will have an impact on future premiums.

Perhaps the greatest worry to an employer is potential liability; the largest direct costs usually come from lawsuits filed by injured employees or the estate of the deceased. Civil suits are becoming more common: It is estimated that out-of-court settlements averaged roughly $500,000 a case. If this sounds expensive, the cost of going to trial is worse: The average verdict is $3 million (Wiscombe, 2002). Even if the company wins the case, there are still substantial attorney fees, associated court costs, and expenses related to the innumerable management hours needed to prepare for trial. Civil suits for workplace violence are less common, but domestic violence is becoming a serious workplace concern.

If you are not yet convinced that domestic abuse poses a serious threat to employers, consider this: The supervisors of Francesia La Rose knew that she was in danger in early 1990. It was made palpably clear to them when her ex-boyfriend called and threatened to kill her if she were not fired. The very next day, he carried out the threat: He arrived at the office where she worked and murdered the woman who had tried to escape his abuse. Some precautions had allegedly been taken by the company, but lawyers representing her parents successfully pointed out in the ensuing civil trial that they were inadequate. It was reported that the family received $850,000 in the wrongful death case (*LaRose v. State Mutual*, 1994).

In a later chapter, we will look more closely at the subject of civil litigation for workplace violence. The primary argument for monetary damages will usually be that the company was negligent in preventing the incident. A company's vulnerability lies in employee-friendly juries who might hear testimony that there were repeated warnings, a lack of response from management, and eventually a tragic event. So many abusers who commit workplace violence end their own lives; survivors tend to turn their frustration and anger to the most accessible and wealthiest target—the employer.

The Occupational Safety and Health Act and laws governing discrimination also provide the legal authority on the issue. Fines can be imposed by the Department of Labor for safety violations should there be injuries. If the abuser is a co-worker or a supervisor, sexual harassment charges can easily be drawn up (and defended) if victims regularly encounter derogatory comments and abusive or hostile behavior from co-workers.

The dipping bottom line is more likely to come from the intangible, long-term effects that a violent incident has on a company. The surviving co-workers will most likely be distraught and thus use more sick leave or even quit. It is easy to understand how the turnover rate of employees increases after a tragic event. The general low morale among those who do stay will seriously impair a business's ability to return to normal.

What about the other vital people? It will be hard to measure the direct impact on the clients and investors, but some of this will appear in the revenue reports, as well as the newspapers and television reports. The public will be reluctant to go to a retail or service establishment where such horrifying violence has occurred. (Consider your own inclination to stay away from an entertainment venue or a family restaurant where there was a multiple homicide that made the headlines in the evening news.) Any indication of the company's culpability or negligence will also lead to a drop in investor commitment and possible withdrawal of funding.

But let us go back to the employee-victims: Most of the expenses related to a violent critical incident will be connected to the victim and the witnesses (another type of victim), largely dependent on how they are treated before and after an incident. The extent of sick leave, loss of production while at work due to poor morale and/or concentration, disability-related costs, and the most expensive concern—lawsuits—can be very low or excessively high, depending on how well management treats the victims. Some security professionals and law enforcement officers pay much more attention to the abuser in order to prevent more violence, but it is crucial to remember the victim. If warnings and pleas for protection are ignored or they are not taken seriously during the investigation and assessment process or the response after an incident is inadequate or insincere, victims and their families will have little sympathy when they return with an attorney to seek monetary damages.

Consider the full impact (direct and indirect) and you can easily see how just a few minutes of rage can drive a small or even mid-sized company to bankruptcy. We have tried in this chapter to describe what domestic violence in the workplace actually costs, but perhaps the greatest cost—loss of morale— cannot be put on a spreadsheet. The emotional turmoil is etched in the memory of those who were there and survived, and in the collective memory of the organization. Survivors often feel denial, anger, guilt, fear, and depression, depending on their experience and character, but everyone will be affected in some way at work and in their personal lives. The invasive recollections of the assault, the resistance to return to the crime scene, and the general effect on sleeping, eating, and social patterns are predictable and debilitating.

Consider also the impacts related to the abuser's life. There will be similar performance problems: poor concentration due to their obsession over the victim, and missed work because of court dates and even jail time. The employers will not be pleased to learn that the abuser has been making threatening calls using a company phone or has or is using a company vehicle to stalk their victim. A more ignorant manager might dismiss this as a marital problem, but in reality, the employee is using company resources to commit a crime (and is being paid for his time, too). Should the abuse escalate to an actual assault, the company might have to share some culpability. Did it provide resources and services used in connection with the crime? Did management ignore any obvious warnings? Was the company directly notified of possible danger? All these things increase a company's liability. This risk multiplies itself if the victim and abuser are co-workers: If the two parties were once romantically involved, sexual harassment laws will still be in effect. Recognizing, understanding, and addressing the issue of batterers in the workplace will be covered elsewhere in this book.

Conclusion

No business leader can afford to ignore the frequent and graphic reports of workplace violence committed because employers and managers did not pay attention to threats made to individual employees. Every business leader has an obligation to protect their workforce from such harm.

But it is the silent impact—the effects of domestic abuse and harassment—that seems to come with greater and cumulative business consequences. Employers must overcome their reluctance to interfere in such so-called personal matters, because the reality is that *employee performance is affected.* Moreover, performance changes are warning signs or pre-incident indicators to management that there might be a violent incident. It is much easier and cheaper to address a problem when it is first recognized; you will be saving a valuable employee from dismissal or self-termination, and your action might well be saving the lives of you and your employees.

The rest of the book is devoted to the task of recognizing, responding to, and preventing domestic violence in the workplace.

Chapter 3

The Dynamics of Domestic Violence

The abuser in an abusive relationship tries to exert control over as much of the victim's life as is humanly possible—control over their relationships, their behavior, their decision-making, their mind, and even their very being. The abuser is driven to maintain power and control over the victim, and wants her to suffer and struggle in order to pacify his own hostility.

The subject of domestic abuse is an extremely complicated one, embracing issues far beyond the scope of this book. In this chapter, we will focus on the basic information every employer and supervisor should know about the dynamics of an abusive relationship, and the role a job plays in the lives of the victim and her partner. We will also address one of the hardest aspects of the subject to understand: why an individual who has suffered so much stays with or returns to an abuser after a violent episode.

Victims come from every age and ethnic group, religion, educational level, background, and income group. Domestic abuse is an equal-opportunity disease that affects men as well as women. Homosexuals are also victims of domestic abuse, and they bear the additional burden of discrimination based on lifestyle and sexual orientation, thus compounding the feeling of alienation and resistance that already exists to disclose their predicament or seek help. Contrary to popular belief, domestic abuse takes place even in highly affluent households: Men and women holding powerful executive or political positions have physically abused their spouses or partners, and professional women and men have been on the receiving end as well. Unfortunately, women with high-paying jobs or social status tend to be more reluctant to get help from agencies or even to report a violent incident to police, out of embarrassment or fear about what people will think. Whatever the personal circumstance, every victim of domestic abuse and violence needs the empathy, encouragement, support, and respect of others if they are to end the cycle once and for all.

Why doesn't she just leave?

It is normal to wonder why anyone would stay in an abusive relationship. Before going on to discuss how domestic violence relates to the workplace, this question should be considered. Certainly co-workers will wonder why the victim doesn't just leave when it is clear that it is a violent relationship. Even the most seasoned victim advocates ask this question. The fact is that unless you have personally been through the experience, you won't truly understand the dynamics of the abusive relationship. Not only do you have to be in their shoes, you need to *be* them as well. This means having their personality, their upbringing, and their perception of themselves and the world around them. Let us say at the outset that within the category of known abusers are women as well as men and within the category of known victims are men as well as women. Any references to one or the other in this book reflect statistical prevalence only.

But we can and should try, because once we examine the tremendous barriers, both internal and external, we might begin to understand why leaving is not so simple. First, if the victim leaves the abuser, she or he is probably giving up an income. This could dramatically alter their lifestyle, and child-rearing and living arrangements. The victim will surely face disapproval of family members and perhaps their religious community. There will be complications over property ownership and child custody. Many abusers threaten a custody battle or clean out the bank account, or even deliberately destroy the family's credit rating. Then there are the prodigious internal barriers of just not feeling capable of living alone. An abuser's initial objective is to break down the victim's self-esteem so that she starts to believe that she cannot survive without the abuser. In the most debilitating cases, the victim even feels that she *deserves* such abuse. Many victims survive on pure hope, believing that love will change the abuser and that things will eventually get better.

The Power and Control Wheel model in Figure 1 helps define the concept of domestic abuse, graphically demonstrating how an abuser exerts control over a victim until the thought of leaving becomes inconceivable. She faces pressure from parents (where perhaps abuse was accepted) and from the community as a whole, as well as personal insecurity.

Figure 1. Power and Control Wheel

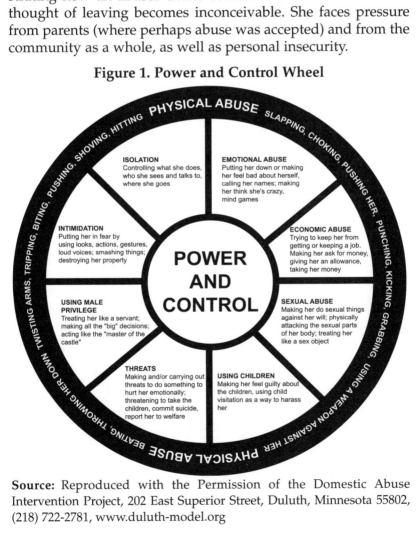

Source: Reproduced with the Permission of the Domestic Abuse Intervention Project, 202 East Superior Street, Duluth, Minnesota 55802, (218) 722-2781, www.duluth-model.org

If you're still trying to understand how a victim can choose to remain with an abuser, consider this: She is afraid she will die. All too frequently, the abuser attempts to kill the victim if she tries to leave. The victim has been told this over and over again, and there is no reason to doubt it. The media barrages us with news reports of situations when this promise has been carried out. This threat, illustrated on the heavy, outer ring of the Power and Control Wheel in Figure 1, dominates and fosters all the other means of control.

The Cycle of Violence

Here is another model that illustrates the dynamics that lead to the decision to remain with or return to the abuser.

Figure 2. The Cycle of Violence

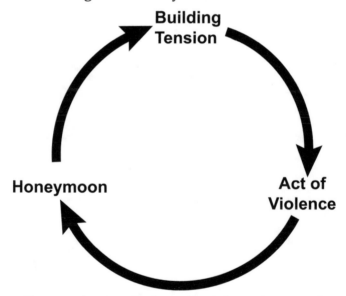

Source: *The Battered Woman Syndrome*, (2000), by Dr. Lenore Walker. Used with permission.

As this model shows, physical abuse is not always a continual element in the relationship. It might start with a night of constant terror, or might be as quick as a single blow. Afterwards, there is usually a period of contrition and remorse, especially if there are pending criminal charges. An abuser will beg for forgiveness and make promises never to do it again. *I was drunk. There are pressures at work. I'm emotionally unstable. I was depressed.* He probably tells her that he needs her desperately. The victim feels confused and truly *wants* to believe the abuser. Still scared about what happened and apprehensive about another incident, she is looking at the man she fell in love with and remembering the good times. This is when he convinces her to forgive him and drop criminal or civil charges.

Unfortunately, this peaceful stage is more likely to be followed by a period of brewing tension. The criticism will return with a gradual increase in the volume and level of hostility in the abuser's voice. The situation will become more tense, despite the victim's efforts to pacify the abuser. Finally, the violence returns, often even more physical and traumatic than before. The process starts all over again, but this time the "honeymoon" period will become shorter and shorter until the abuse is the predominant element of the relationship.

This cycle of violence rarely stops on its own. If the abuser is to understand and stop this behavior, he will have to actively and willingly address the issue, most likely through treatment and counseling. While it is possible for a healthy, loving relationship to eventually evolve through these efforts, the victim must put her own safety (and that of her children) first. There is a window of opportunity, right after a violent episode, when the victim will often give serious thought to leaving. It is at this point when co-workers and supervisors are key to helping victims achieve safety and freedom from abuse. Supervisors and HR staff members do not have to take on the role of counselor; they can simply show support and concern, provide the opportunity for the victim to make these changes, and refer them to other helpful resources. This way, the victim can take back her life, and the employee can return to work and achieve optimal performance for the company.

It is important to realize that offering support to victims of abuse is not about splitting up couples or breaking up marriages. It is about ending the abuse. Often a victim must leave for their own safety and the safety of their children long before the abuser understands the nature of his actions and chooses to change.

What can an employer do if the victim chooses to remain in the abusive relationship? If the victim decides to stay, the best thing an employer can do is to foster a supportive atmosphere and make referrals to appropriate sources. Let the victim know that time off will be allowed for court and other appointments (e.g., counseling) and that you will provide additional security. These things can convince the victim that the workplace is a resource (when there are few other options). If their job is secure, the biggest economic obstacle facing them will be gone because they will have an income, and this might encourage them to take the necessary measures to protect their own well-being.

Employers need to understand the cycle of abuse. In the course of helping an employee, the victim is probably going to return to the abuser, despite extensive and generous measures offered by management. This can be frustrating and quite incomprehensible, but you don't have to understand why they went back: You just have to concentrate on how *you* can help this individual in trouble and protect the workplace. Employers must be consistent and reasonable in the allowances they make for all of their employees, but they need to think through a decision before acting on it. Firing the battered employee or pressuring or requiring them to leave the abuser in order to keep their job is putting up yet another roadblock, limiting their ability to make choices and find independence.

Domestic Violence and Self-Esteem

The relationship between domestic violence and employment is complicated. Many victims cannot keep a job because their abuser schemes to get her to quit or be fired in order to exert more control. If the victim has the strength to leave, the abuser will try to take away any part of the victim's life she or he has rebuilt. Incidents that occur at work, ranging from telephone harassment and verbally abusive arguments to disruptive scenes in front of others, are the abuser's attempt to damage the victim's work life. They are tactical ploys that exert and maintain power and control. The employer who takes the time to understand the needs of the victim and the abuser will help the victim overcome the many obstacles that keep her in the relationship. We will explore these factors next.

SELF-ESTEEM

Perhaps the most important element that employment offers to offset the damage done in an abusive relationship is the opportunity to raise a victim's self-esteem. Having the money to acquire needed and wanted items, feeling a sense of accomplishment in a job well done, and having colleagues and supervisors show appreciation and respect will change the way a victim of domestic violence sees herself or himself. The abuser can insult, criticize, blame, and generally diminish the victim's ego, but employment gives the victim the most fundamental benefit of all: the reassurance that they really do deserve better.

Many victims realize that they are not being treated fairly but lack the confidence to leave or stand up for their rights. Some even believe that they deserve the abuse. An abuser is at the height of their control when their partner is demoralized into believing that she or he cannot possibly survive out in the world without the support and guidance of the abuser. Many victims are literally prisoners in their own homes, but others who are able to work are compelled to return to their hostile home environment by mental and emotional "bonds" that are just as strong as any physical ones.

Self-esteem is a person's belief in their own intrinsic value. It acts as the encouragement to seek a new life, free from abuse. Above all else, victims need to believe that they have the strength to reject another person's violent and abusive control and move on to create a new, independent, and rewarding life.

INCOME

Money is the great liberator. It allows us to travel and gain access to a greater range and quality of services, and dramatically increases the array of options available to us. Many victims do leave their abusers, only to be faced with financial obstacles that are too great to overcome. Consider the costs of moving under adverse conditions: security deposits on an apartment and on utilities and telephone, days of lost work, and moving expenses such as the cost of renting a truck or hiring a moving company (if the abuser hasn't destroyed all of the victim's property). Add to that the sudden change in family income, childcare, custodial arrangements, and lifestyle and we just begin to comprehend the challenges. If there is court action, legal fees alone can wipe out any hard-earned savings. Having productive employment provides the resources to make leaving an abusive relationship possible.

The abuser wants to do more than simply control the victim's income so that she cannot leave. How money is spent is also a crucial issue of power: Often an abuser will take control of all the money the victim makes in order to further control her life. If the victim has to ask for money to buy groceries, clothes, or gas for the car, she will be inherently dependent on the abuser. Victims usually have to hide and hoard any loose change, just to provide for essentials (though this will put them in serious jeopardy if they are caught). With employment, there is some chance of keeping a little from each paycheck and holding out to have some control over this crucial aspect of their lives.

Many abusers go to great length to ruin the victim's credit, especially if the two are married. "Bad debt" is jointly owned, and can further reduce a victim's ability to become independent.

Many victims who try to leave or make it on their own fail because of financial constraints. A paycheck can offer a sense of hope and a way out. An employer who continues to support battered employees is really investing in their future. What does the employer get in return? Devoted loyalty and sincere dedication—two things that have value well beyond the dollar figure.

JOB SKILLS

A paycheck is not the only benefit of employment. A steady job is the first step toward better career opportunities. Should a victim leave the abuser and move to another state, a long and steady work history on a résumé makes for a more qualified and attractive applicant. Even with an education and needed work skills, many victims have trouble finding another job because of their sporadic work history. As the cycle of abuse illustrates, victims can experience brief periods of employment and long stretches of unemployment during the abusive episodes of the relationship. Clearly unable to explain these gaps to a potential employer, a victim must make shallow excuses or duck the question when asked. Maintaining a solid employment history makes the victim a more attractive candidate and can persuade the current employer to keep them on.

Employers help abused workers support themselves and create a stable work history, but they make another valuable contribution: When the victim works, she is learning valuable job skills, which makes her more marketable. Whether it is learning new computer software programs, becoming more confident in handling purchasing and shipping arrangements, or even developing important business contacts, a victim employee is stretching and learning to become more proficient in the industry or profession. Some positions are highly specialized, offering the chance to pick up competitive skills that can even lead to certification and licensure. Promotion and salary increases are now possible, thus making it easier to leave the abusive relationship.

Preventing the victim from building job skills might not be the immediate objective of the abuser, but it is to their advantage to impede the development of the victim's job skills. Knowing this makes some employers even more determined to provide those learning opportunities.

Perhaps the most important job skill that can be directly applied to leaving an abusive relationship is the ability to problem-solve and multi-task. The myriad challenges of any occupation provide a testing ground for the victim to practice overcoming the obstacles they will face when they try to leave. By completing the tasks at work, they gain confidence and use the same skills they will need to find new living arrangements, work with law enforcement agencies, and present a solid case in court.

SOCIAL INTERACTIONS

Abusers usually begin their emotional manipulation by trying to isolate the victim from other people. Friends, family, neighbors, and anyone who might give the victim support or encouragement are seen as threats to the abuser's sense of control. The fact that the victim is leaving the house at all to be surrounded by and to interact with other people is often a great source of consternation and jealousy for the abuser. It is quite common to be suspicious of and accuse the victim of having an affair, even if the name of another man comes up in their everyday conversation.

Why is social contact important? The first advantage is that it changes how the individual sees herself. Victims are often criticized and denigrated daily, until their self-esteem withers away. Co-workers and supervisors are able to bolster their ego by offering praise for their accomplishments. This can offset the negative messages the victim hears at home about herself, and can change her self-perception.

Co-workers provide significant practical help. An encouraging co-worker might learn of the abuse and become that one supporting friend who can offer understanding and faith—especially if she or he has experienced the same trauma and has managed to leave the abuser. This type of support is invaluable, not only because of the empathetic understanding, but also because the victim will know that it really is possible to escape an abusive relationship. All managers and supervisors should be informed about the situation so that they can refer the victim to appropriate resources if there is an appropriate opportunity. This can be followed by much-needed logistical assistance and legal protection (all of which will be covered at length in subsequent chapters).

Be aware that workplace support might upset the abuser. However, the greatest threat will come from their paranoia that the victim will find another partner. A sense of ownership over the victim is at the core of how the abuser views the relationship. The chance that the victim is having an affair or flirting will drive the abuser to demand an exact accountability of the victim's every movement, and it is this jealousy that is the source of the most dangerous and malevolent behavior (and a key motivation for violence in the workplace). Many victims who died at the hands of their abusers were told, *"If I can't have you, no one will."*

TRADITIONAL ROLES

The king of the castle and the obedient and subservient wife are common stereotypes present in most abusive relationships. The idea of a woman earning an income and contributing to the household economy is offensive to an insecure male. It might be enough to drive an abuser to force his partner to quit or to get her fired: this will secure his position as the sole bread-winner and satisfy his own ego in a warped sense of male dominance. It should be noted that even if both people work 40-plus hour shifts and come home at the same time, the woman is still expected to accomplish all the household chores of cleaning, cooking, caring for the children, and being an attentive, dutiful wife. When she falls short (and who wouldn't?), the abuser has the excuse he's looking for to "punish" the victim.

Work provides the victim with a change in atmosphere (away from the abuse), but it also offers a different view of how men and women can interact—and, perhaps more importantly, it shows her what she is capable of accomplishing.

A note here about cultural diversity: Our ethnically diverse society has made us look more carefully at gender roles, but whatever family structure and household customs exist, it is never culturally acceptable to abuse a partner. Whatever responsibilities or characteristics adults take on in a family, using a religious creed, ethnic tradition, or cultural value to violently dominate another person is a warped excuse if there ever was one.

Conclusion

A job is worth much more to the victim than just the paycheck: Maintaining employment can very well be the key that leads a victim to find freedom from abuse. Understanding their situation and supporting them on the job can protect a victim and provide the means toward a safer and healthier life. In return, you as employer are likely to get years of dedicated and productive service.

To gain a better understanding of the dynamics and issues of domestic violence, consult any of the numerous resources available on bookstore shelves, on the Web, and through community advocacy agencies. Some links to Web sites appear in the appendix. Advocates who staff local shelters and agencies can provide professional expertise as well as discuss the problems relating to family violence within the local community. Most domestic violence agencies have training programs for volunteers, and some will be able to provide your company with training and consultation. This collaboration will greatly benefit both the agency and the company. More importantly, it can provide the crucial link for victim employees who need the support.

Chapter 4

What If the Batterer Is Your Employee?

Chances are pretty good that every employer at some time or another will be handing a paycheck to at least one individual who stops off at the local pub for a few hours, gets drunk, and goes home and beats his spouse or partner. There are no statistics on the exact number of batterers and abusers there are in the country's workplaces, but the number of victims on record indicate that the U.S. total would be quite significant. There are many good reasons why employers must pay close attention to this reality.

Abusers as well as victims have a direct impact on every organization that has a workforce because they are *in* the workforce. Employers who prefer to hire men because they assume that they won't have to deal with domestic violence issues are in for a rude awakening. This chapter explores the problems related to the batterer employee, whether it is a man or a woman. Let's start with some basic questions.

If an employee batters his wife while they are away on vacation, should his supervisors be concerned? Do they have the right to investigate? What if the trauma is severe, putting his wife in the hospital? At what point does it suddenly become an employer's business? If the woman subsequently dies of her injuries and he is charged with manslaughter or murder, would he keep his job (assuming he posted bond, pending the trial)? Would he be re-hired after a short prison term? What if the victim is also an employee at the same company? Should this change how management views the situation? Finally, what if the assault takes place during work hours, and on company property? Is it still just a personal or marital issue?

Abusers who have been convicted of manslaughter or murder will likely be in prison for a prolonged period of time, making the issue of whether or not to keep them employed moot. It is the more-common simple assault cases that employers need to think about. What policies and protocols exist for employees who are convicted of violent crimes? And would the company's response depend on the functions of their job or their status in the company? What about employee-batterers who continue the abusive behavior during work or who use company equipment or resources to do so?

Prevalence

As we mentioned, there are no studies that tell us definitively how many abusers there are in the workplace, but the sheer frequency of reported violence indicates that it must be a significant number nationwide. Documented studies of law enforcement and hospital records indicate that there are hundreds of thousands of assaults on victims reported every year. It is obvious that it is not the same handful of abusers committing such acts. Domestic violence has a direct impact on every business that has employees, no matter the gender.

Again, the assumption that men are the abusers and women are victims is not absolute. Women can victimize their male partners just as heinously.

Type of Job

Are there certain industries or professions that attract or perhaps even develop men or women who commit domestic abuse? The stereotype is that those who are in blue-collar positions or engaged in manual labor or physically strenuous activities are more likely to be violent with their partners, but recent research suggests something different: In 2002, University of California research sociologist Scott Melzer studied the correlation between abusers and their occupations. He examined the professions of abusers who were committed to treatment programs to see if there was a higher prevalence of abusers in certain lines of work. Using abusers who worked in white-collar, management positions as a baseline, he compared these men to the men in other professions to see if there were higher or lower rates of abusers in those professions. Perhaps one of the most interesting of findings was that men who were in traditionally female-dominated positions (such as office clerks and classroom aides) were 47 percent *more* likely to commit acts of domestic violence. Somewhat more predictably, men who worked in violence-prevention fields (such as law enforcement or prison security) were 42 percent more likely than an office supervisor to assault their intimate partner.

Further research is needed to confirm any speculations, but it appears that there is a natural connection between the violence that law enforcement officers and prison guards experience at work to the high levels of physical stress and a higher tendency to abuse their domestic partner. The connection between female-dominated occupations and the prevalence of abuse by men who choose these jobs does take some supposition. However, the researcher suggests that society's expectations of what a man should be doing professionally adds additional stress that is later expressed at home in the form of abuse. (One might infer that this prejudice and perceived ridicule leads to the abuse, not any particular characteristic of the work that they do.) Whatever this study demonstrates, it is crucial to remember that *domestic violence is committed by people of every level of income and education.* There might be more men who are ordered to enter abuser-treatment programs who have less education and lower-wage jobs, but it is more likely that better-paid individuals are able to avoid such consequences through better legal representation and other means.

Job Performance

The impact of the abuse on a victim's job performance is reason enough to warrant an employer's concern, but the behavior of the batterer on the job deserves just as much attention. After all, if the victim is being harassed and threatened during work hours, the abuser is making those calls in that time frame. Additionally, an abuser's attention to his work is affected by what happens at home; perhaps he continues the abuse while at work, or dwells on it. This takes him physically or mentally away from his job responsibilities.

This issue of the batterer's impact on production was examined in a small study sponsored by John Hancock Life Insurance Co. and published by an organization called "Employers Against Domestic Violence in Massachusetts." The principal investigator, Emily Faith Rothman, surveyed men participating in a batterer's treatment program, and was able to obtain frank and surprising discoveries regarding the "other side" of domestic violence in the workplace. Oddly enough, even though participants chose to engage in the abusive behavior, almost all spoke of how they suffered emotionally long afterward. Obsessed with what their partner might have been doing, the workers were not able to concentrate on the job. Mistakes were common.

It is difficult to gauge the extent to which companies are affected by a batterer's lack of focus, but every employer should be concerned. Almost all of the participants who had access to a company phone admitted to using it to "check up on her." Couples often call each other at work, but we are not talking here about a friendly hello. These men said that they called only to intimidate or monitor their partner to see if she was doing something she was forbidden to do (i.e., socializing with other men).

One man related this: "I would call her to see if she's at home. How many times she would be on the phone calling whoever and how long she was on the phone with each person and how long it took her to answer the phone. 'How come you were on the phone with your friends? Are they more important than me? Huh? F*** your damn friends, huh?' She would be on the other end of the phone and if the phone rings three times and all of a sudden she clicks in ... I [knew she was talking with someone else]. I would use my [work] phone to do that probably four times a day."

The stalking behavior described by these men also consisted of the use of company computers to send e-mails and company vehicles to check on their partners at home or at work. Carrying out personal errands on company time is frowned on, at best. What is to be said of committing criminal acts such as harassment and stalking on company time? Or using company vehicles or equipment? The offenses are compounded when, as some participants in the survey reported, they recruited co-workers to help them monitor the victim.

You cannot possibly know what your employees are thinking about and you cannot watch their every movement, but you should notice absenteeism because it might be a direct result of abuse. On average, the participants in this study missed approximately seven full work days dealing with the justice system. Whether they were in criminal or civil court, were meeting with attorneys, or were being transported to the magistrate's office in handcuffs, *they were not at work.* Those who reported that they never missed a *full* day's work said that they were out an average of 20 to 25 hours a month, just dealing with the fallout from their behavior.

Perhaps the most egregious revelation was what the men said about how the employers responded to their behavior. The vast majority of supervisors offered support to an employee who admitted abusing a partner, and a few said that their supervisors went so far as to post bond when they were convicted. Rarely was there any consequence for their behavior, unless it was tied to substance abuse. In those cases, the only stipulation was that the employee was to stop drinking and get counseling for that behavior; the violence was not mentioned.

To follow up on what the Massachusetts study revealed, the North Carolina Council for Women and Domestic Violence Commission initiated a similar study. They encouraged partici-pants in batterer-treatment programs to fill out an anonymous survey so that they could identify workplace repercussions and gauge the response of the participant's employer. Out of 188 completed surveys, a surprising 81 percent of the batterers stated that they were employed during the time they engaged in the abusive behavior. Even more alarming to an employer should be the fact that 25 percent of the offenders were working for the same company as the victim. This drastically increases management's responsibility and liability, as the abuse and harassment rarely stops once the shift starts or when the two are on company grounds at the same time.

When the Victim and the Abuser Are Co-Workers

Having a batterer in the workplace becomes a much more complicated problem when both the victim and the abuser are employed by the same company. As problematic as this might be, it is actually fairly common. If the company is one of the major employers in a community, several generations of a family have probably worked there. Also, there is always the possibility (and opportunity) that two co-workers will become romantically involved. While many such relationships are healthy and wholesome, a certain number eventually turn sour. The rate of divorce and the tentative aspect of dating leads to a higher probability that the two individuals will eventually not want to work together, side by side. Add the complications of "triangle relationships" and affairs, and one can see how troublesome the situation can become for other employees and for productivity. When these complications become disruptions, you have a nightmare on your hands.

What if there is an unequal relationship between the victim and abuser? The company can be charged with sexual harassment if the abuser holds any sort of supervisory or management authority over the victim. The dynamics of the abuse will surely have an effect on performance evaluations, duty assignments, and even the continuity of employment. The victim will be especially vulnerable to the abuser because he or she can exert yet another layer of control. Some companies prohibit personal relationships between supervisors and employees in order to avert any possible ethical dilemmas. Known couples can be separated so that the employee has a different supervisor, or can work in a different division. Some company policies require that this be done.

But how risky are intimate relationships between employees? Are they, in themselves, precursors to workplace violence? Thousands of such liaisons are present in organizations, and too many of these romances turn catastrophic.

Consider the 2002 tragedy in an Oakland, California Safeway grocery store. Jorge Barosa and G. B. were allegedly having an affair, though she was technically his boss. They were apparently together for about a year before she decided to break it off. He transferred to another store and seemed to be getting on with his life, until he showed up at her store to talk to her one morning. It was not strange for him to visit, and so nobody was concerned when they talked outside for a while before returning inside. Then he pulled out a revolver and shot her in the back of the head. After killing his ex-partner, Jorge then turned the gun on himself.

On the other side of the country, another tragedy shocked the workplace not long after the California incident. An executive in a major insurance company based in New York killed the woman he had been having an affair with when she tried to end the affair. According to newspaper sources, John Harrison, an ex-FBI agent, had just taken over as head of the insurance company's fraud department when he allegedly became involved with one of the workers. He left his family to pursue the relationship, but when his girlfriend decided that she did not want to continue with the affair, Harrison refused to accept it. He pursued her, despite her resistance. According to a police source, she sent him an e-mail that read, *"You need help. You're sick. Leave me alone."* Her judgment of his mental state was accurate: One morning Harrison called the woman and a co-worker into his office and shot and killed them both. It is unclear what relationship he had with the other victim, but Harrison apparently had his reasons. After shooting them both numerous times, he then turned the gun on himself.

Would a no-dating policy have prevented such occurrences? There is some debate as to the effectiveness of such rules. Interested parties will come together despite policy or wedding vows. It is much more effective to put your energy and effort into raising awareness and creating a supportive environment where employees feel safe to come to management with their concerns.

But what kind of abusive behavior occurs while they are actually working? There were only a limited number of reported incidents. The majority of participants were in the program per court order, so they might not have been entirely honest in their responses. However, at least 14 percent admitted to having used company equipment to harass their victim. Other abusive behavior reported included calling the victim when warned not to, calling the victim's employer in order to get the victim in trouble, confronting their partner at work, and going to the victim's workplace despite being prohibited.

There was limited data on how employers reacted to the news that the abuser was committing such acts while at work. Most abusers in the study did not know if their employer was aware of the situation and 10 percent of the respondents were certain that their supervisors knew nothing about it. Half of the employers in these cases who were aware of the abuse failed to take action. In only one case did the employer warn the employee that something was being done.

The impact abusers have on the workplace was made clearly significant through a more recent study by the Maine Department of Labor and Family Crisis Services, an advocacy agency. By compiling the survey response of 152 participants in different batterer intervention programs, they were able to describe a picture that would raise the eyebrows of any employer. In terms of jail time alone, 70 respondents in this study indicated that they missed work as a result of being arrested. The combined time lost from work was 15,222 hours, which translated to about $200,000 in financial costs. Even when they were at work, these abusers often were not doing their job. Over three-fourths of them described how they used company resources such as the telephone or company vehicle to contact or visit their victim. While it is not unusual for an employee to call home during the day, these messages and visits were specifically made to express their anger or to harass or even threaten their victims.

Even if the victim is never at the job, there is still likely to be trauma, if not violence. The survey revealed that the workers were distracted or unable to concentrate on key safety concerns because they were thinking about the victim. In one situation, a worker knocked down a pile of heavy material while driving a forklift. In another, a man was seriously burned by mistake when he mishandled an explosive substance. In a near-miss incident, one worker actually cut through his safety chaps with a chain saw. Accidents can and do happen, but these participants in the treatment program knew why they were distracted: They were thinking about controlling their victim. When they were at work, they were unable to know and to control what their victim was doing, but it remained the focus of their thoughts. Job safety was not on their minds.

What is clearly evident is that an employee's abusive behavior is rarely addressed. It is not a matter of whether management approves, cares at all, or is concerned about the acts of violence. It should concern management that (1) *paid time* is being used to commit crimes; (2) company resources are being used to carry out the crimes; (3) the batterer's focus and concentration are reduced (thus reducing productivity and possibly posing a safety risk); and (4) the employee-abuser will probably not be on the job for extended periods of time.

Handling Co-Worker Situations

Any acts of abuse on the job, including threats and harassment, need to be considered acts of workplace violence. The hostility committed by one employee against another, even though the two are married or living together, needs to be reported and investigated. Managers are reluctant to get involved in or to meddle with a couple's private affairs, but this can be a serious mistake. A workplace violence policy cannot have exceptions: Even when the employee victim does not want management to intervene and discipline the abuser, such actions simply cannot be ignored.

If all of the abuse occurs off company grounds and after work, an employer would have less of a responsibility to address the issue, but the company cannot pretend that the abuse is not taking place. The impact on the victim will most likely be obvious. The same support and protections should be offered to this person as would be offered should the abuse take place at work.

There is even more responsibility placed on the organization if the victim comes to management to report his or her fears. Inadequate response to such a report can result in costly and embarrassing litigation should the prediction come true.

Liability Issues

Undoubtedly, the most expensive costs of having an employee-abuser are related to liability. In many eyes, an employer is responsible for the actions of an employee. This might seem unfair, but as a rule, the organization is obligated to prevent foreseeable acts of violence. Legal settlements of these cases average in the hundreds of thousands of dollars. If a case goes to trial, a jury verdict can reach into the millions. (Chapter 5 addresses legal issues in more detail.) Let's turn now to some areas of concern should the abuser be an employee.

SEXUAL HARASSMENT

Just because the victim and abuser has or had a personal relationship does not mean that the employer is immune to charges of sexual harassment. Every organization with more than a handful of employees is wise to have an expressly written policy on the subject. Hundreds of cases every year point to the employer's responsibility to maintain a work environment free from sexist comment, harassment, and sexual battery. When the victim and abuser work together, nearly every act of abuse, control, intimidation, and violence will fit within the parameters of the Title VII Sexual Discrimination employment law, which addresses the employer's responsibility to maintain an environment free from sexist comment, harassment, and battery. Once the employer is aware of the harassment, he or she has a well-established obligation to remedy the situation.

Whether the victim works with the abuser or not, an act of violence that leads to injury will create a liability for the employer of the perpetrator. The basis of these lawsuits is the plaintiff's claim that the business was negligent in the management of its employees. In very simple terms, companies can be found liable if an individual is injured and the employer knew about or *should have been aware* of the violent actions of their worker. This is generally broken down into negligent hiring, supervision, and retention.

NEGLIGENT HIRING, NEGLIGENT SUPERVISION, AND NEGLIGENT RETENTION

Negligent hiring often revolves around the business's failure to fully investigate the background of an individual before he or she is hired. In some positions (such as security jobs), the employee is trusted with vulnerable clients or sensitive information. It is imperative that anyone hired for such roles has a clean record, free of criminal or questionable activity. Many businesses have lost expensive legal suits filed by a customer or client who was assaulted by the company's employee who was involved in a domestic abuse situation. If an abuser's job gives him special capabilities or authority (such as the ability to track individuals or carry a weapon), the employer cannot be too careful when it comes to hiring.

Negligent supervision refers to the employer's failure to monitor the activities of an employee. Employee-abusers often engage in stalking and harassment on the clock. The employer might not care to know what their employees are doing every minute, but he might be a little upset to learn that the abuser was using a company vehicle to follow the victim, or using the company's privileged access to information in order to track down the victim (who could be trying to escape the abuser). These are behaviors of serious concern. Consider the power and capabilities of the Internet: An employee using a company computer and ISP service to track, locate, and then send threatening messages can easily engage in such behavior without the company's knowledge.

Negligent retention, probably the most incriminating of the three, refers to a situation in which the employer was warned or knew of the potential for threat but did nothing to try to prevent the violence. There are countless cases where victims called the abuser's employer to beg them to intervene and no action was taken. Only when the employee in question is arrested for assault or even murder does management consider their failure to respond.

In truth, there is very little research done on the civil suits filed regarding employer liability for employee-abusers. Increased public awareness of domestic abuse and a more litigious society makes it imperative that employers take precautions and reduce their risk. Ignorance can no longer suffice as an excuse; the public, the media, and the court system all know it is the employer's responsibility.

One final note: Businesses generally want the public to take them seriously, and they like attention. Brand naming, market placement, and customer familiarity are the objects of marketing and sale efforts. But what if a potential client's first thought when he hears a company's name is that it was identified on the news as the employer of a man who killed his wife and two children, and then committed suicide?

Prevention

Employers have tools and means to prevent and address the issue of employee-batterers. They can increase awareness and prepare the workforce to avoid a tragic event and the resulting lawsuits. It starts with policy.

POLICY

A workplace violence policy is a mandatory document in every sizeable company, and domestic violence must be a component. The policy must clearly note any prohibited actions that will not be tolerated when committed against anyone. Many policies are designed to prevent employees from harassing, threatening, assaulting, or battering fellow co-workers, but this prohibited behavior should be enforced to protect everyone. Clients, vendors, contract workers, the public at large, and the employee's friends and family can be expressly identified as well. After all, it is the behavior that is prohibited—it does not matter to whom it is directed.

OFF-DUTY BEHAVIOR

There are situations where even off-duty conduct needs to be considered. In the North Carolina State Personnel Manual, there is a paragraph attesting to this very subject.

> An act of off-duty violent conduct may also be grounds for disciplinary action, up to and including dismissal. In these situations, the agency must demonstrate that the disciplinary action, suspension, or dismissal is supported by the existence of a rational nexus between the type of violent conduct committed and the potential adverse impact on a State employee's ability to perform the assigned duties and responsibilities. (North Carolina State Personnel Manual, Workplace Violence Policy)

Essentially, if an employee's position and job responsibility are highly sensitive, he or she bears additional accountability. Inappropriate or criminal actions off the job still call into question a worker's ability to carry out his or her job, especially when the individual is in a security position or has counseling or mental-health responsibilities. How can an individual be trusted to protect employees or to provide nurturing support if he or she has been victimizing a battered partner? It may require the actual conviction on a criminal charge or even a permanent restraining order to verify that the violent behavior occurred. Otherwise, it would be very difficult and perhaps inappropriate for a company to investigate something that happened off-grounds and not on company time. As we shall explain in Chapter 9 on Policy Development, company legal representatives should be consulted when drafting language surrounding the abusive behavior of employees.

Managing an Abusive Employee

The first step in managing an employee-batterer is to know that he or she has a problem. Look for problems with job performance and absenteeism, and any sign of injuries related to the victim's attempt at self-defense. But much more likely, there will be no indication that the employee is beating his wife once a month. It is not uncommon for the identified abuser to be considered a great guy, friendly, and amiable to all. It is his or her charisma and charm that often makes people doubt the veracity of the victim who makes allegations of abuse.

Employers sometimes only realize that there is a problem when the individual is caught making a threatening call, or when the victim comes to the employer seeking help in getting him to stop. Very often, it is only when the abuser calls from jail (seeking help getting out or to explain their absence) that the issue is revealed. The response will vary, depending on how management finds out and what the offense is.

When a clear violation of policy has been identified, every company has the ethical and practical responsibility to act. Take the example of a victim who tells a supervisor that the abuser is following her for extended periods of time and is driving a company car: A deeper investigation proves that he indeed is falsifying driving records to spend inordinate amounts of time tailing and monitoring his victim. The supervisor might be reluctant to interfere in this highly emotional and personal issue, but the inappropriate use of company resources needs to be addressed, just as it should be if an employee is taking two-hour naps in a parking lot. The same disciplinary consequence would need to apply, despite any of the abuser's explanations.

Sometimes, the abusive behavior is more sinister and troubling. The victim might show a supervisor an e-mail from the batterer that is laced with obscene, virile language in which he makes direct and terrifying threats. A check with the information technology department can verify that it was sent from his computer and maybe even from the company's e-mail server. This is now an outright crime. Whether the victim chooses to take out a warrant is beyond the company's control, but the company has a responsibility to do something about the message. While companies are often lenient about the occasional personal use of e-mail to send a joke or send a message to family members, communication of this caliber cannot be ignored. The workplace violence policy and disciplinary procedures need to be applied.

DISCIPLINE

The abusive action may require immediate termination, but management should also consider such options as demotion, suspension, and/or a reduction in pay. There will be arguments against firing the batterer right away, the most vocal of which will probably come from the victim. If the batterer loses his job despite the fact he chose to do what he did, he may still blame the victim. *"Look at what you made me do"* is a frequent statement abusers make. The firing might destabilize the batterer even more. With loss of employment, there would be further complications that would frustrate and infuriate the abuser. Perceiving to have lost it all (their victim/partner, their job, and then their car, home, and security), a perpetrator might be pushed over the edge to commit the most extreme form of violence. A large percentage of domestic homicides are followed by a suicide.

The decision as to whether or not to fire someone, given the possibility of this reaction, is a difficult one that many employers have had to make. The solution is best arrived at with the help of a team of professionals and outside consultants who can help you weigh all the options. The safest path must be considered, as well as what is right. Termination should be done only when safety measures have been assessed and implemented for the protection of the victim and the workforce.

REFERRALS

If the employer decides not to terminate, disciplinary action might not get to the root of the problem. If the employer wants to try to rehabilitate the employee, the employee assistance program can do an initial assessment and refer the individual to the appropriate resources. In the absence of such a program (or in conjunction with developing an action plan), management will be faced with an array of choices.

Businesses must be aware of which actions that have not worked in other situations and that might even aggravate the crisis. Domestic violence is not about poor impulse control, so do not suggest sending an employee to "sensitivity training" or a class in "anger management." Domestic violence perpetrators are often rational, careful, and well aware of how they are trying to dominate their victim. It is not about losing their temper in a moment of frustration: It is about the abuser's frustration at not being in complete control. In many cases, much of the abuse is done when the abuser is calm and composed. If the problem were poor impulse control, the abuser would be hostile with everyone (they would yell, threaten, and strike co-workers, clients, and perhaps even supervisors). Hostile and impulsive workplace-violence perpetrators do exist (more on that later), but a large percentage of domestic violence abusers are considered to be normal, everyday people. Charming and personable, their aggression is reserved for only one person—the victim in their control.

Try not to consider it a marital problem. Almost all couples have problems, and all have a mutual responsibility to maintain harmony and partnership in a relationship. Domestic violence, however, is a crime about power and control. To refer this couple to a marriage workshop or marital counseling is to suggest some culpability on the victim's behalf. While these counseling sessions may address the feelings of anger, frustration, jealousy, and resentment, they are not designed to identify and confront the violent and threatening behavior. Often, these sessions are manipulated by the abuser, who places guilt on the victim by identifying her behavior as the source of the conflict.

However, there are resources that are applicable. Treatment programs just for batterers address this behavior for what it is: an effort to control and dominate a partner. Knowing this is the key to confronting the abuser with what he is doing. The majority of participants in such programs are forced to attend as conditions of a court order. Failure to finish the program would result in incarceration, and this is the main reason for their attendance. An employer can put similar conditions on an employee when termination is not an immediate consequence, but there must still be some positive change in their behavior at work. The success of these programs generally relies on the participant's own acceptance. If he recognizes his actions as wrong and realizes his own motives in such conduct, there is a greater chance of change. Being forced to attend a program for batterers in order to maintain a job or to stay out of jail does not ensure that he will take responsibility for the abusive behavior. He has to accept it as a way of taking personal responsibility for his problem.

RESTRAINING ORDERS

We will outline the various legal options open to employers in the next chapter, but let us take a look at special issues regarding co-worker relationships.

A restraining order prohibits the abuser from even coming within a certain distance from the victim. This can certainly impact working conditions if both people are employed in the same building. It has to be clear that the onus for obeying the restraining order is completely on the perpetrator. It is his or her responsibility not to approach, contact, or even be within the vicinity of the victim. The abuser's livelihood will be jeopardized, and he or she might plead this issue during the court hearing. While the judge can impose special conditions on the order, the safety of the victim will be the primary focus of the decision. The company does not have any court mandate to separate the two parties, but it alone has the ability and the power to arrange the schedule and work duties to ensure that the stipulations of the order are carried out. Separate discussions with both parties can lead to a solution so that both people can do their work with no opportunity for interaction.

Managers have to be vigilant in making certain that the abuser does not cross the line of his court order. Phone calls, e-mails, inter-office mail, and actual visits should be monitored and recorded as evidence of violation. The abuser might try to work around the stipulations of the order by soliciting help from co-workers to check up on the victim; such activity demonstrates that the perpetrator has no regard for authority, cannot keep to commitments, and is still bent on continuing the abusive behavior. You must watch for this and take immediate action.

By no means should the victim ever be forced to change time shifts or locations unwillingly, just because the abuser does not want to make such changes. If the abuser is never required or is not asked to make adjustments and the victim is being asked to make them, there will certainly be grounds for a grievance against the employer. Furthermore, it sends a very dangerous and negative message to other workers that abusers will not only be tolerated, but might even be given preferential treatment over the victims.

Unfortunately, in a great many cases, management will not get to make the decision because the victim simply quits, rather than face a confrontation. In a North Carolina case, the abuser and his victim were both waiting tables at a popular chain restaurant, working similar shifts. The boyfriend assaulted his girlfriend in the restaurant parking lot after work one night in the spring of 2000, but management did nothing to discipline the employee. After the victim obtained a restraining order and told management of the legal restrictions the order placed on her boyfriend, she was asked what she intended to do about work. It was implied that her only option was to call the police if he was at work at the same time. Her supervisor and many fellow employees felt that it was unfair for him to lose his job, because she was the one who obtained the order to protect herself. The woman decided to quit. It was apparent that management favored the abuser's employment over hers and made no effort to change the employee-abuser's schedule. Whatever legal recourse the victim had was beyond her capabilities, emotionally and financially. A number of community activists were so perturbed by the manager's action that they stopped eating at the restaurant. It fell just short of becoming a public relations nightmare for the restaurant, which faced a community-wide boycott and no doubt paid dearly for its actions.

Workplace Violence Indicators

If you are an owner or a manager, you must identify an individual's risk to the workplace. Many of the people who committed horrific acts of workplace violence against co-workers and supervisors had a history of domestic abuse. Some abusers offer no threat to their co-workers and management, but how do you determine which ones will? Management should be concerned with the propensity for violence and a willingness to use it to maintain control. Some abusers are considered "nice guys" who do not have violent tendencies. The truth is that there are so many people who commit abuse, it is impossible to pigeon-hole or stereotype them. Many are relatively harmless to all except their victim. Others are a danger to us all.

In one of the worst cases of workplace violence ever documented, Mark Barton killed his wife and his children in 1999 before going on to kill nine people and wound 13 others at two Atlanta brokerage firms. He was the primary suspect in the murder of his first wife and his mother-in-law years before, though his guilt was never proven.

In a California case, Joe Ferguson killed three co-workers and a bystander after killing the woman who tried to leave him.

In Virginia, the wife of Peter Odinghizuwa took out an emergency restraining order against him after he allegedly assaulted her, but others later had reason to be afraid of him: In early 2002, he killed two teachers and a fellow student at the Appalachian School of Law, and injured three others.

In February of 2000, Tracy Moss suffocated his ex-wife and his girlfriend before he went to his workplace and murdered his boss. Police surrounded him after a chase, and he turned the gun on himself.

In one of the most baffling cases, postal worker John Taylor killed his wife in 1989 and then went to the postal facility in Escondido, California, where he worked in order to continue his killing spree. He shot three co-workers, killing two of them. He was not the troubled, disgruntled employee one would expect; he was considered a model worker and had earned several perform- ance awards. There was apparently little indication that he was having any trouble with his job or his work relationships.

Would an awareness of the abusive and violent tendencies of these individuals have helped prepare owners, managers, and co-workers for the violence? Violence-prevention experts generally agree that the more managers know about the history of aggression and what a perpetrator is capable of doing, the better they can assess their own risk. So should this information be obtained *before* an employee is hired? What is the value of pre-application screening?

Many professionals in the field of workplace security emphasize the importance of properly screening applicants. What about potential employees who have a history of domestic abuse? The frequency of such behavior suggests that it would undoubtedly shrink the interview pool. Before consid- ering the merits of identifying previous domestic violence as a risk to the workplace, review another recent case of workplace violence: In South Bend, Michigan, 54-year-old William Lockey killed four co-workers and wounded two others. Could this tragedy have been predicted? Years earlier, Mr. Lockey was committed to a mental institution for an incident that was potentially even more deadly: After making threats to kill his wife (at her workplace), he attempted to kidnap their baby. His plan was to use the baby as a hostage, take control of the county jail, and gain entry to the courthouse tower (where he had stashed supplies and over 2,500 rounds of ammunition). From his perch in the tower overlooking the entire town, Lockey intended to hold the town hostage and kill as many people as he could. Law enforcement intervention during his baby- snatching attempt thwarted his despicable plan, landing him in the institution. However, his inclination to commit mass murder reappeared 34 years later, when he killed his co-workers at the manufacturing plant.

The correlation between an individual who is willing to commit atrocious acts of violence in the workplace and domestic abuse deserves further study, but we may never completely understand how the workplace or a person's domestic life motivates a person's desire to kill. When an individual uses violence to make a partner obey their will, do they employ the same tools of fear and brutality to get what they want from their employers or exact revenge? As you can clearly see from this anecdotal review, an abuser is a violent person. This alone necessitates the concern of everyone around them.

Conclusion

In the majority of situations, what an employee does in his or her own home is not a company's business. Nevertheless, many human resource professionals know all too well that people bring their personal conflicts and issues to work. Abusers will have trouble at work, whether from their behavior while at work or from their inability to be at their job due to court or jail. It is not just the loss of production that can impact the company: An employee-abuser's behavior can be squarely blamed on the business that provided the tools of the abuse, especially if it was aware of the danger or risk and ignored it. In the most critical and lethal cases, domestic violence has a deep and devastating impact on their workplace, whether or not the abuser is an employee.

The problems associated with domestic abuse seem daunting, but employers can take clear, simple, and effective steps to reduce their risk and create a safer work environment, as we will see in the next few chapters.

Chapter 5

Legal Issues

Just what are the mandates and regulations imposed upon a company to protect its employees and facilities? There are federal and legal directives for each state that must be followed explicitly or there will be grounds for steep fines and lawsuits. It is not within the framework of this book to list each state's constantly evolving laws, however. We will instead cover broad national mandates, as well as trends at the state level. It is a key responsibility of every owner, manager, and supervisor to become familiar with how these policies govern and direct the relationship between employer and employees.

In this chapter, we will broadly categorize the laws into one of three main areas: laws regarding protection of the workplace; laws protecting the rights of employees; and the legal options employees and their families have if they are injured or killed at work.

The Work Environment

OSHA

The primary law outlining what protections businesses are required to provide to employees and their customers is known as the Occupational Safety and Health Act of 1970 (OSHA 29 U.S.C. § 654(a)(1)). This broad and far-reaching law basically establishes an organization's responsibility to ensure a safe work environment. The general duty clause reads as follows: *"Each employer shall furnish to each of his employees employment and a place of employment which are free from recognized hazards that are causing death or serious physical harm to his employees."* The U.S. Department of Labor governs this federal mandate; each state has a corresponding department, as well.

Several things must be considered when it comes to violations. First, there must be a threat or hazard in the workplace that is grave enough to risk death or serious personal injury. Many victim employees trying to escape their abusers have had to deal with this threat on too many occasions. Not only is the victim at risk, but the managers, co-workers, customers, and even the public at large are potential targets.

Next, the hazard must be recognized as a *hazard*. There is some room for debate as to whether or not an employer is responsible for failing to recognize the danger risk if management was never notified. If the situation involves domestic violence, most of the threatening behavior has probably taken place in the victim's home or at least away from work. The embarrassing and isolating nature of abuse makes a victim reluctant to disclose their situation, so one can reasonably argue that the employer could not have known about the threat. However, this can be challenged if the abuse comes to the workplace through harassment or actual visits by the batterer. Consider the case of an employee who witnesses the threatening behavior and reports it to a supervisor or a manager: This notification is then determined to meet the standard for a recognized threat. If a supervisor witnesses the troubling behavior, he or she will have additional reporting responsibilities. If a victim of abuse warns management of potential danger, the hazard is considered to be clearly recognizable.

The employer's responsibility to be aware of threats made against employees should not be shirked. Violence can often be prevented, and the business will not be as vulnerable to claims of liability as it would be with the trauma and tragedy of a homicide. Employers must take reasonable measures to reduce the risk of a violent incident, including having an effective and well-developed threat-assessment team to manage these cases.

The senseless and tragic incidents that continually assault our workplaces can never be completely prevented, and the most extensive and resource-laden measures are not always necessary. The best thing to do is to assess *every* situation to determine the appropriate course of action. The worst thing an employer can do is to ignore the situation, because this is when liability and actual risk are the most damaging to the company.

OSHA violations come with hefty fines—up to $7,000 per violation. Financial impact, however, should be the least of your concerns: If it is determined that there was willful and intentional neglect of the threat, those employers and companies declared responsible face prison terms of up to a year.

As of January 1, 2002, companies are required to keep a record of assaults made on employees by former or current intimate partners, just as with any other injury. The nature of the injury has to be such that it requires medical attention. This new requirement will add to the list of ways that domestic abuse affects business.

CIVIL PROTECTIVE ORDERS

Civil protective orders are used with varying degrees of effectiveness. Also known as *peace orders, domestic violence protective orders,* or *restraining orders,* the primary function is to stop the perpetrator from contacting or coming near the victim (and possibly their children). The workplace can be listed on such orders.

There are usually two stages: The first is an ex parte "order to emergency" order that can be obtained almost any time and the defendant (abuser) does not have to be present during the court proceeding. The order usually lasts for ten days, during which time the court order will be delivered and the individual will be informed of the next court date. This is the second phase: The abuser will be allowed to defend the charges against him or her. If the court finds in favor of the victim, the order will be extended and enforced for one to three years, with opportunities for renewal. There is no requirement to have an attorney represent either party.

But what does this mean to a business? The responsibility of staying away from the victim is placed on the abuser, and there are no specific employer obligations. Actually, a protective order can be a useful tool for employers in the development of their safety plan, because it provides a way to stop any harassment that impedes a victim's job performance. The protective order can spell out that the abuser is not to contact the victim in any way; management can assist the judicial process as soon as possible following an incident by documenting and saving any messages conveyed by phone, e-mail, or other means. Security or front desk personnel should be given a copy of the restraining order if police have to be called because the abuser has arrived at the workplace.

The situation becomes more complicated when the abuser and victim work at the same location, most particularly if they are on the same schedule. Sadly, some judges will exempt the workplace from protection, thereby jeopardizing the victim or forcing her or him to quit. While it is the abuser's responsibility to stay away from the victim, the employer is sometimes stuck in the predicament of deciding whom to move where. Accommodations can be made to help both parties meet the requirement of the order, but by no means should the victim have to be jeopardized in terms of schedule or employment in order to comply. An employer who forces a victim to resign in order to meet the conditions of a restraining order sends a message to other victims of abuse that management will not support them, and also unwittingly lets abusers know that their actions are condoned. Such an environment fails to foster loyalty and sends employees a message that they are not so important after all.

A note of warning: There have been many cases where employers have demanded that the employee-victim obtain a restraining order if they want to keep their job or advance in the company. This infringes on the victim's right to self-determination and can even aggravate the situation, acting as an impetus to violence.

Workplace Restraining Orders

Waiting to see if an employee takes out a restraining order will be frustrating to the employer who clearly recognizes the potential threat and is suffering from the harassing behavior of the abuser. After all, even though the direct focus of the abuse is on the victim, the entire workplace and company productivity are affected. Human resource professionals have been lobbying in a growing number of states for "workplace restraining orders" to reduce the risk of workplace violence, and they are becoming more common.

What is a *workplace restraining order*? In essence, it is a restraining order that prohibits an individual from stepping on company property. It allows a business owner to obtain the same degree of protection that domestic restraining orders offer, but it is the employer rather than the victim who takes the perpetrator to civil court and requests relief from a judge. Such orders can be used against any credible threat to the workplace, such as ex-employees or disgruntled clients. This remedy can place the same type of restrictions on the defendant: he or she would not be allowed to contact, come within so many yards, or in any way disrupt the facility or the employees of the business.

In some states, statutes specify that an employer can take out the order for the entire workplace, in which case the defendant will not be allowed to make contact with *any* employee. In other states, only the identified employee-victim is protected. The requirements for such remedy are easy enough: You have to prove that the perpetrator is a credible hazard to the workplace because he or she has made previous threats or there have already been incidents that intimidated or injured one or more employees. However, some states are more stringent, requiring proof that the victim is indeed an imminent or dire threat of serious injury or death. That's not always possible.

The process of obtaining a workplace restraining order is fairly simple: An attorney is not required, and there is usually no fee, but since it is a legal proceeding, it is wise to seek advice and assistance from the company lawyer. One advantage of a workplace restraining order is that it gives the employer the opportunity to be proactive in addressing a batterer's behavior. It also takes the blame off the victim because it is their boss who is taking the abuser to court, not the employee. The victim won't have to face the abuser in court and testify to all the embarrassing details.

There are many things an employer should think carefully about before taking out a workplace restraining order. Most of all, employers should be wary about making the employee-victim participate in the process. You don't want to scare others from reporting their own tenuous situations. Even more dangerous, this step might further aggravate an irrational, vengeful person into taking drastic measures. Employers need to take precautions whether or not they obtain workplace restraining orders, as we will explore such actions in subsequent chapters.

CRIMINAL CHARGES

The restraining and trespass orders fall within the arena of civil court. If these orders are violated, it becomes a criminal matter. However, abusers very often engage in criminal behavior when they are under protective order. Any warrants for threatening or violent actions made against the victim must be taken out by the victim or an officer, but when there are damages to a business, the company might be the plaintiff. If an abuser breaks or defaces company property, for example, the employer can press charges directly through the magistrate's office or with the help of law enforcement. If the abuser is causing a scene at work, the authorities can come and arrest him or her for disturbing the peace. While the statutes generally have the same language and intentions, the title of the law and other specifics vary considerably from state to state. It is best to work with local police to determine what actions are appropriate and most effective, given the specific behavior. Incidents that cross state lines or international boundaries might constitute violation of federal law.

Victim Rights and Employment Law

Whether the incident takes place at work or takes place somewhere else, there are employment laws that offer protection from negative repercussions by an employer. A victim might have to be given time off from work and the employer might have to make other reasonable accommodations. Employer obligations vary from state to state, but certain federal mandates apply to all 50 states. Furthermore, once a victim decides to file a complaint or seek support through one of these remedies, an employer must be careful not to take any form of *perceived* retaliation. Any negative employment action, such as denying a promotion or a training opportunity, giving a negative evaluation, or creating what is perceived to be a hostile work environment can be considered an unfair response to an employee's attempt to seek relief from these sanctioned remedies. Fair-business practices and thorough documentation are crucial to ensure that false claims are not substantiated.

Victim Rights

There are a growing number of state laws that specifically protect victims of domestic violence in the workplace. So far, New York, Maryland, California, Illinois, and Rhode Island have general policies that specifically identify the workplace rights of victims of domestic violence. Certain states do not allow an employer to discriminate against a current or potential employee solely on their status as a victim of abuse. These laws might also protect a victim if they need to take time off from work to attend to court or medical appointments by, say, imposing penalties or providing grounds for a civil suit if an employer disciplines or fires an employee for this reason. New legislation is being introduced each year as the issue of domestic violence captures the public's attention. More business associations are standing up against domestic violence, and there is more educational outreach in the form of seminars and workshops. Employers must be proactive in adopting these policies before they become mandates.

THE FAMILY AND MEDICAL LEAVE ACT

Known by the acronym FMLA, the federal Family and Medical Leave Act prevents an employer from firing or getting rid of an employee because of a personal medical crisis or trauma. For employers with at least 15 employees, up to 12 full weeks of unpaid leave are provided to any worker who has a serious medical condition. Billions of dollars are spent on health care every year to treat victims of domestic abuse: the victims frequently use up all their sick leave due to the abuse, so the FMLA is important worker protection.

The health costs related to domestic abuse are huge. A large majority of emergency hospital visits are made by women who were beaten by their partners. Their injuries often require lengthy stays in the hospital, only to be followed by weeks of physical therapy before they are able to return to work. However, physical injury won't be the only reason why these women will need time off. The FMLA provides protection for workers dealing with any serious physical and psychological health condition, such as depression and/or post-traumatic stress disorder (PTSD). These traumatic conditions, which are just as debilitating as physical injury, are likely outcomes of the continuous and cruel mistreatment that the victims experience. An employee suffering from either of these symptoms might have to obtain a note from a physician saying that the individual is unfit for work duties. The Family Medical Leave Act protections cover the family members of an employee as well: If an employee's daughter is a victim, for example, the employee will be allowed to take time off to care for her in the event that continual care is required. Considering how prevalent it is for women to be physically and emotionally traumatized by an abuser, it will not be unusual for employees to ask to leave work to be at the bedside of a loved one who has been battered.

The FMLA goes even further: It also covers an employee's leave if he or she adopts a child or must provide foster care for a child. In the resulting turmoil that abuse creates (or in the event of a death of a mother), the grandparents are usually the ones identified to care for the children. Domestic violence is prevalent in every state, and its related costs can debilitate companies and the economy as a whole.

An employer does not have to pay the employee while he or she uses the FMLA option, but must hold their position in case they return within the allotted time. Meanwhile, work goals are not met, the remaining staff has to take up the slack, and temporary help might be needed. The obvious proactive solution is to provide support and protection to victims and hold abusers accountable *before* a worker needs to take lengthy time off from work. With early assistance, the risk of abuse can be minimized—which might in turn minimize the need for time off.

AMERICANS WITH DISABILITIES ACT

The effects of domestic violence are often extreme enough to disable a victim, yet not enough to make them incapable of employment. The Americans with Disabilities Act kicks in when the injury substantially limits a major life activity. Some injuries from physical abuse can permanently change a person's ability to function the way they could before the assault, perhaps keeping them from performing activities such as lifting, carrying objects, or even sitting in a chair for periods of time. However, some individuals are still able to carry out the functions of their job if reasonable accommodations are made by the employer. Wheelchair access or modifications to their work routine might be all that is needed to maintain employment. (See 42 U.S.C. § 12111(9); 29 C.F.R. § 1630.2(0)(2)(I-ii): "EEOC Enforcement Guidance: Reasonable Accommodation and Undue Hardship Under the Americans with Disabilities Act.")

The mental or psychological injuries are just as debilitating. Depression and/or post-traumatic stress disorder can affect an employee to the extent that their job performance wanes. However, it is possible to accommodate the victim by providing counseling and making adjustments so that the employee can still carry out his or her responsibilities.

The court system realizes that employers need workers who can do their jobs and honestly earn their pay. Reasonable efforts to accommodate their needs should not impose undue burden on a company—the employee still has to be able to do the job. The ADA protects workers from an employer's knee-jerk reaction to simply dismiss an employee who suffers from trauma, physical or emotional. If an employer feels unduly burdened by this mandate, he should be reminded that the positive efforts a company makes to help a traumatized or abused employee can produce lasting benefits in terms of workforce morale and loyalty. What might look on the surface as a drop in an individual's productive "value" will be far outweighed by the support and increased productivity demonstrated by an appreciative workforce.

It should be noted that the Americans with Disabilities Act usually does not protect the abuser who makes an ADA claim to prevent their own job loss. The abuser might have documentation from a physician or a mental health professional indicating that the violence or threatening behavior is due to a personality disorder or a side effect from medication, but the reality is that an abusive employee is unlikely to win such a case. The courts have found that an employer's duty to protect his or her employees and customers overrides a disability that exhibits itself in threatening or violent behavior. It is also considered a worker's responsibility to refrain from threatening co-workers or clients.

Discrimination Title VII—Sexual Harassment

Federal and state laws protect employees who have been sexually assaulted or who receive unwanted advances or even experience verbal abuse. An employer must maintain a non-hostile work environment, as determined by the U.S. Supreme

Court in 1986 in the *Meritor Savings Bank vs. Vinson* case, where a manager of a bank made repeated unwanted advances to an employee. The bank was found liable for the manager's behavior (despite the fact that the victim and the manager had a prior social relationship). In this precedent-setting domestic violence case, management was found to be unlawfully harassing an employee.

Companies must establish clear and active policies and procedures to address sexual harassment in the workplace, and must be especially careful when there are personal relationships between supervisors and employees. Employers are mandated to maintain a work environment that is free from sexual harassment from anyone, including clients and people not associated with the business such as boyfriends or partners of employees. The company must prevent or stop any kind of sexual harassment. It centers on the issue of discrimination: Women make up the majority of victims of domestic violence and sexual assault, and employers who allow a hostile environment to exist or who fail to make allowances to address the needs of a victim may be found guilty of sex discrimination (and subject to fines and liability claims).

Unfair disciplinary action taken against a victim is also addressed in law. For instance, if male employees are allowed to take time off to tend to their personal matters or are given support when there was injury or illness, yet a victim of domestic abuse is not, the employee-victim can file a grievance with the Equal Employment Opportunity Commission. When there is no legal justification for such unequal treatment, the employer might have to face a discrimination lawsuit. Very often, victims are fired from their jobs due to their abuse often because the injured or battered employee's appearance is unsettling to clients and co-workers. The employer, perhaps concerned that the abusive situation will get complicated, might want to avoid any "trouble." Terminating an employee who otherwise demonstrates positive work performance is opening the doors to possible litigation because any discrepancy in treatment among employees can constitute or appear to be an act of discrimination. Defending one's company against such discrimination charges will be costly and time-consuming.

PUBLIC POLICY

Finally, disciplining or discriminating against a victim of abuse might constitute a violation of public policy. State and federal laws protect employees who are pressured by employers to break the law or who are denied time off for jury duty. They also shield victims who are trying to seek justice.

A pending case in Massachusetts is expected to result in a landmark decision on discrimination. On July 29th, 2000, a newspaper reporter was assaulted by her partner. That evening, she left a message with her supervisor that she would not be able to come in the following Monday. On that day, she went to court to seek an extension of her restraining order and to testify in criminal court about the assault and violation of the temporary restraining order. She also went to the police station to be photographed for evidence (injuries to her face), and she changed the locks on her doors at the recommendation of the police. That afternoon, she spoke with her supervisor and told them that she would return to work the next day. When she arrived on Tuesday, she was told that she was fired, allegedly due to her absence. Her wrongful-discharge case was initially dismissed by a lower court, but with the support of the NOW Legal Defense and Education Fund, her claim was appealed to the Massachusetts Superior Court, which ruled that the case could move forward.

The ruling contained this passage; *"The public policy interests here are primal, not complex: the protection of a victim from physical and emotional violence; and the protection of a victim's livelihood. A victim should not have to seek physical safety at the cost of her employment."* (*Apessos vs. Memorial Press Group,* No. 01-1474-A; 2002 Massachusetts Superior LEXIS 404 [Massachusetts Superior Court], September 30, 2002.) Regardless of how this case is ultimately resolved, it will set a precedent that every employer must be aware of before he or she terminates an employee simply for seeking protection (as is their right as a citizen).

Compensation for Injuries

Let's say the worst occurs and a victim is actually assaulted and injured on the job. The employer will probably have to pay for medical bills, as well as wages and other expenses. Especially in cases where fatalities occur, compensation might include multi-million-dollar punitive damages. Was the employer aware of the threat? Is or was the perpetrator an employee? How negligent was the employer in protecting employees? All these factors help determine who the court will favor and how much monetary compensation will be awarded.

WORKERS' COMPENSATION

Basically, Workers' Compensation covers medical and mental-health expenses and lost wages that are incurred should an employee get hurt at work. It can also cover funeral expenses in the event of a death. The extent and type of financial support will vary from state to state, but generally Workers' Compensation is designed to cover the expenses that result from an employee's injury or death, while protecting employers from extraneous lawsuits. In general, this benefit is the only way an employee can obtain relief for their injuries. They are usually not able to sue their employer to compensate for the harm done.

Workers' Compensation is available to most employees who are injured on the job, but there are stipulations: Was the incident a result of the person's work? For instance, let's say that a clerk in a convenience store is shot during an armed robbery. The clerk's responsibility is to handle the cash and tend the store, and these responsibilities led to the assault. The important factor for the employee to obtain this benefit is that the incident occurred "in the course" and "arising out of" their employment.

This is a pivotal factor in situations where an abuser comes to the workplace of the victim and inflicts injury or death. Essentially, the personal or romantic relationship of an employee usually has no connection with the actual business of the company: The assault might have taken place while the victim was working at their place of work, but the motivation or reason for the incident was completely removed from the nature of the victim's work. In other words, the assault had nothing to do with their job.

One tragic case illustrates this issue poignantly. Janice D. believed that she was starting a new life, free of abuse. Her ex-boyfriend had stalked and harassed her to the point where she needed to seek psychiatric help and obtain a restraining order. She now had a new job working as a clerk in a convenience store. On June 21, 1996, she was startled to see the man she had fled from waiting for her to ring up his six-pack of beer. After paying for the beer, he threw the six-pack at her, striking her in the chest. When he left, she pleaded with her supervisor to call the police—she knew her life was in danger. Janice was told to continue working, despite her desperate fear. Shortly thereafter, her ex called her on the phone and said that he would kill her if she hung up. She discreetly begged her supervisor to either call the police or allow her to leave. The response was for her to hang up the phone and get back to work. Her supervisor insisted that the man would not come back and Janice needed the job, so she stayed. She was still in the store when the ex-boyfriend returned with a handgun. He shot her three times. Fortunately, she survived.

When Janice applied for Workers' Compensation benefits, her employer and the company's insurance carrier denied her claim. She took it to the State Industrial Commission, but they upheld the denial. Her final appeal went to the North Carolina Court of Appeals, which ruled that while the incident occurred "in the course of her employment," it did not "arise *out of* her employment." Workers' Compensation benefits were denied because the assault was entirely unrelated to the nature of her job duties! In citing a previous case, the assault was a "personal risk that the plaintiff brought with her from her domestic and private life" and that the motive that inspired the assault "was likely to assert itself at any time and in any place" (*Dildy v. MBW Investments, Inc.,* North Carolina Court of Appeals, August 6, 2002).

What if the victim and abuser work together? If they are just co-workers, it can be argued that the victim was assaulted just because he or she was an employee. However, if they had an outside relationship, it was the downturn of the interpersonal relationship, rather than the professional or occupational one, that lies at the root of the aggression. In another recent North Carolina case, an ex-partner murdered a victim at the place where they once worked together. While the victim's Workers' Compensation claim was denied, benefits *were* granted to a supervisor who witnessed the assault and suffered from post-traumatic stress disorder. The logic of this argument can only be described in the legalese jargon of a courtroom.

These decisions sound unfair for employees, but denial of benefits might actually help victims and harm the employer. If an employee is awarded benefits under Workers' Compensation, he or she would not be able to file a lawsuit. The exclusivity of Workers' Compensation as the sole remedy plays a crucial role for both the victim and the employer in domestic violence incidents. While Workers' Compensation only applies to lost wages and expenses, a lawsuit can be much more detrimental to a company because it will allow for punitive damages and claims for emotional distress. In short, if the victim is able to collect Workers' Compensation, they will not be able to sue. If the victim is denied this benefit, they will be able to file a claim in civil court.

CIVIL SUITS

What is often the deepest fear of any employer is to be brought into a courtroom by the family of a deceased employee. This is just what happened in an Oregon Supreme Court case, as court records show:

> Chris Blake and Achara Tanatchangsang worked on the same shift in their employer's Pertiand manufacturing plant. Blake and Tanatchangsang were also involved in a romantic relationship that ended in November, 1995. In January, 1996, Blake told the employer's plant superintendent that he was having difficulty coping with the breakup and that he did not

want to work the same shift as Tanatchangsang. The employer's plant superintendent approached Tanatchangsang and offered to transfer her to a different shift. Tanatchangsang did not want to be transferred, however. In January, 1996 and again in March, 1996, Tanatchangsang reported to her supervisor that Blake had called her derogatory names. At some point after the March, 1996 incident, Blake was placed on medical leave.

In April, 1996, while still on medical leave, Blake entered the employer's manufacturing plant and shot and killed Tanatchangsang while she was at work. He then killed himself.

Panpat vs. Owen-Brockway Glass Container, Inc.
49 P.3d 773,334
(Oregon Supreme Court, 2002)

At issue was whether or not Workers' Compensation was the sole remedy for the victim's family to seek compensation. In order to prove that it was, the employer had to show that the incident occurred in the course of her work, and that it arose out of her employment. There was no contention that the murder occurred at work; the issue was *why she was shot*. Even though they worked together, the reason was a personal matter that had nothing to do with the responsibilities of their job; it was the end of their off-duty, romantic relationship that was the motive for the assault, not a dispute over work assignments or envy over a job promotion. Therefore, the estate of the victim was allowed to seek monetary damages from the company through a lawsuit.

This does not necessarily mean that every litigant will win their lawsuit against a company for failing to protect an employee from assault, but the possibility of losing civil and third-party lawsuits is of primary concern to business owners. Some attorneys might advise that having a protocol and policy regarding domestic violence in the workplace might actually increase the risk of liability. Stated policy or no stated policy, the real risk of litigation is when management is negligent when notified of a potentially violent incident.

To substantiate a claim:

▲ There must be clear warning signs indicating the likelihood of the incident.
▲ The employer must have been made aware of these signs.
▲ There were reasonable actions that the employer could have taken to prevent the act of violence, but the employer failed to take those actions.

Was the assault foreseeable? This is pivotal. The pre-incident indicators (previous occurrences in the workplace, threats passed to management, direct warnings from the victim) have to be reasonably blatant to prove that the employer should have known that violence might occur in the workplace. If there is sufficient evidence, civil action can be based on a variety of issues, such as failure to warn or protect an employee(s) or liability for causing "wrongful death."

In another case (*LaRose v. State Mutual Life Assurance Co.*, No. 9322684, 215th District Court, Harris County, Texas, 1994), the family of the victim received a substantial settlement in the wrongful death action against the victim's employer. As the suit explained, Ms. LaRose's supervisor received a call from LaRose's ex-boyfriend, advising that if LaRose wasn't fired, he would kill her. The very next day, he followed through with his threat. Although security had allegedly been warned and had prepared for an incident, the man was able to gain access to the victim's workplace and shoot her to death. The employer was found liable because of the security breach.

In yet another case, a company was ordered to pay $5 million in damages to the families of victims (*Tepel v. Equitable Life Assurance Society*, No. 801363, San Francisco, California Supreme Court, 1990). In this situation, even though the company was allegedly warned that the husband of an employee was a threat to the workplace, it failed to implement effective safety measures. The resulting death of two workers and the injury of nine others led to a liability claim that was based on failure to respond, despite direct warning.

There is liability when an employee is a victim of abuse, but the risk is much greater when the company also employs the batterer. It can be argued that any threat from a personal or home source is not the affair of a business, but the actions of an employee *while on the job* is certainly their responsibility.

These lawsuits are based on three general categories: negligent hiring, negligent supervision, and negligent retention. Most negligent-hiring cases focus on situations whereby a prospective employee was hired even though there was no background check done to determine if the individual posed a risk to co-workers, customers, or the public (or the check was inadequate). In many of these cases, the employee who has a history of sexual assault attacks a client or co-worker. However, in the area of domestic violence, it is rare and unlikely for a company to be sued for hiring an employee with previous convictions. How the employee behaves during work and how he or she is handled once an issue arises is considered more relevant.

"Negligent supervision" applies when there has been a failure on management's part to see that an employee is properly monitored. While it can be argued that an employer cannot possibly watch every move of every staff member, there are aggravating factors that might place more responsibility on a company: Basically, if it is the nature of the job or the company provides resources and access that help a perpetrator be more capable of committing acts of domestic violence, it can increase the company's liability.

For example, an employee at a credit investigation firm uses his authority and resources to track down and stalk a victim, or another example, a victim's ex-boyfriend uses the company's investigative services to locate a woman who is trying to elude him, and he is doing it under the pretense of doing legitimate detective work. The company in each case is liable. It is the *employee* who is misusing the powers and tools vested in him. It can be argued, however, that such potent capabilities need to be monitored to ensure proper usage. The investigative agency and his or her supervisor can certainly be held responsible.

However, the riskiest situation is when management has been warned of an employee's criminal behavior. Judges and juries tend to consider negligent retention to be a most culpable act. Every manager, no matter the size of the company, must be aware of the threats or actions on the part of an employee, and must take proper measures to discipline or prevent further incidents. A case in North Carolina illustrates this: In *Braswell v. Braswell* (330 North Carolina 363, 410 S.E. 2d, 897, 1991), the family of Lillie Braswell filed a negligent supervision and retention lawsuit against the Pitt County Sheriff's Department. The wife of a deputy had gone to the sheriff to express fear for her life at the hands of her husband. She was not exaggerating: several days later, while driving on the highway, she was murdered by her husband. However, the court did not hold the employer liable for numerous reasons: The incident occurred while the deputy was not on duty, and there was not sufficient evidence that the husband was an actual threat. The woman's word was not enough. The Sheriff did send deputies to check on her husband, but their report allegedly stated that their colleague was not a danger.

The fact that the employer did not lose the lawsuit does not diminish the importance of taking the issue seriously. This case went all the way to the North Carolina Supreme Court. The costs of the litigation, the adverse impact on the department's reputation in the community, and the costs to the taxpayers relating to extended court trials all point to severe financial repercussions when employers do not take domestic violence seriously or seriously enough. In essence, no one really wins in this kind of emotional and prolonged lawsuit; it is far better to have policies and programs in place to prevent the incident from occurring in the first place, and to follow them explicitly.

Policy Risks

As we said earlier, a company's legal counsel might advise against adopting a domestic violence policy in the belief that it will increase the liability of a company, should there be an incident. If a business acknowledges that domestic violence is a risk to the workplace yet fails to prevent an occurrence, will this make the company more guilty than a company that never openly recognizes the danger? Being more concerned with protecting yourself from lawsuits instead of preventing actual violence is reprehensible and dangerous on moral and practical grounds. First, it is crucial that you confront the issue of domestic violence head-on and be proactive in preventing it and intervening. Creating a policy sends a clear message to employees that they should talk to managers about the problem and warn them of any pending threat, and that if they do this, the employer will be supportive. Second, it can be argued that the company is taking measures to address this workplace hazard and is making good-faith efforts to prevent it from ever happening. Finally, there is a legal risk of having a policy and not following the policy *as outlined.* Often, the document mandates certain practices such as quarterly training sessions for supervisors, but if the sessions are not actually held, a suit can be made on a breach-of-contract claim. (The company would be making assurances to employees that it did not carry out.) To prevent this risk, only develop measures that will be carried out and review all policies and written procedures to be sure that they contain only the practices that the company is able to commit to and carry out.

Conclusion

The legal issues surrounding domestic abuse and employer responsibilities are somewhat complicated and confusing, even for people who have to deal with such policies on a daily basis. Common sense says to be fair and to document everything. The purpose of this chapter is merely to provide an overview of related laws and discuss trends in case law; when a legal matter arises, be sure you consult with the company's legal counsel, as well as with police, human resource associations, and experts in employment law.

Chapter 6

Communicating with the Employee-Victim

In younger days, I worked as a short-order cook in a Greek diner. I prepared the gyros, and a middle-aged co-worker prepared the salads. We worked closely together in the fast-paced, hot, and often hectic work environment and got to know each other pretty well. When my co-worker started coming in late (and sometimes not at all), it was only her long employment with the place that saved her from getting fired. Some days, she came in with black eyes and swollen cheeks. Nobody ever said anything about her appearance; I assumed that she wanted it that way. No eye contact, little conversation, no explanation. I knew this single woman had a boyfriend whom she supported, and I knew from having conversations with her that he had substance abuse "issues." Rumor had it one week that she had asked for an advance on her pay. She was thrifty and never spent money frivolously, so I figured she was really desperate when she started to borrow money from her co-workers. I thought I was helping when I gave her some. I think I said something like, *"Are you doing all right?"* but she just nodded and thanked me for the cash. Even then, I knew I was not really helping—I just was not sure what to do. She left not long after that, and I hope she finally did meet someone who knew what to say and could show her a way out.

Perhaps you have been in a similar situation. The signs and symptoms may be subtler and less obvious, but a manager who has had years of supervisory experience can usually tell that something is amiss. It might even be apparent from bruises and frequent tears. The truth is that managers and co-workers often suspect an employee of being a victim of abuse, no matter how hard the employee tries to hide it. But even with this suspicion, it is unlikely that the victim will ever broach the subject.

Taking the first step with an employee is one of the most difficult things a supervisor or colleague can do. Of all the responsibilities and duties that a supervisor engages in as a result of domestic violence and its effect on the workplace, confrontation is the task people tend to be the most reluctant about. In this chapter, we will try to address these questions and areas of concern:

▲ Why don't supervisors approach the victim?
▲ What gives you the right or opportunity?
▲ When, where, and how should you approach a victim?
▲ How to listen
▲ How to avoid two common pitfalls:
   – Making judgments
   – Pushing the individual to leave their abuser

Why People Don't Get Involved

There are many reasons why people don't approach someone they believe is being abused by their domestic partner. Among the possibilities are:

▲ Not knowing what to say or how to broach the subject
▲ Fear of being intrusive or of interfering in their business
▲ Fear that you may humiliate or embarrass them
▲ Not being aware of the resources available or ways to help
▲ Believing that the abuse happens in most families and/or that it will pass
▲ Resistance to discuss disagreeable issues or subjects
▲ Reluctance to draw the anger of the abuser
▲ Assuming that the victim is dealing with it or already knows where to go for help

▲ Fear of becoming too involved

▲ Believing that someone else will do it

There is no doubt that this is an embarrassing topic to discuss—especially for two people who don't know one another very well. It is an extremely personal issue, and employers in general try to maintain a business-like environment. If all the conversations are "small talk" and are kept on a polite but social level, how does someone introduce the topic without indirectly implying that something is wrong in the victim's life? You don't want to say something that offends and alienates the other person or get yourself involved in a very complicated and difficult situation, tied up in a cycle of continuing support and dependence. Most people have too much going on in their own lives to be stuck in this dilemma. Getting involved can also mean personal injury or retaliation: the abuser might go after anyone who tries to support the victim or help them leave the batterer. There is also the possibility that the abuser is an acquaintance whose wrath and volatility is well known.

Perhaps the biggest reason why people don't say anything is that they don't know *what* to say and they don't know where to start or how to approach the subject. The silence continues, and the issue not only goes unresolved, but often degenerates.

The best way to approach a victim is to be straightforward. Once the conversation begins, the issue will take over—just follow the natural steps of listening and providing support. It might be awkward at first, but once the subject has been brought out in the open, your sincere concern will overcome any feelings of personal embarrassment.

As a supervisor or co-worker, you can be a friend, but you should not play the role of counselor—this should be left to professionals. It is your decision as to how involved you want to get in the victim's situation, but do set sensible boundaries and take precautions. Community agencies and organizations are adept at handling issues related to domestic abuse, and they are able to provide the services and attention that the victim needs, with less risk.

One very appropriate and objective reason to approach an employee who might be dealing with abuse is that his or her job performance is most likely affected: decline in productivity, occasional tardiness, or increased use of sick leave are all common. In the worst cases, the abuser's behavior warrants the need to discuss the matter—frequent calls at work or visits to the workplace or parking lot are scary, and they disrupt the victim's routine and that of co-workers.

The Approach

Here are the basic components of the discussion:

1. State what you have observed that concerns you.
2. Share your desire to help the individual, and explain what support is available (more details on this in a later section).
3. Finally, just listen.

Confronting the individual might be the most difficult step a manager can make, but doing it at the right time and in the right place and knowing what to say can make it much easier. Carefully consider when you want to hold the discussion. The decision to say something might have been sparked by a dramatic decline in performance or an incident that cannot be ignored. Perhaps there was a scene out in the company parking lot one morning between the victim and abuser. Perhaps the employee has used up all her sick leave, yet called in stating that she cannot come in today. It might be a culmination of smaller things that finally constitute an undeniable problem—perhaps the abuse has reached a very chronic and frightening stage. (She is struggling to survive, and just getting to work is a challenge.) It is in this extreme period that the victim is most receptive to someone approaching them. It might be what they have been waiting for, even subconsciously. Feeling so isolated and bereft

Fayetteville

SOCIETY FOR HUMAN RESOURCE MANAGEMENT

AREA

AFFILIATE OF

HR
SOCIETY FOR
HUMAN
RESOURCE
MANAGEMENT

Please join us on Wednesday, August 27, 2008

Our program topic this month will be Security and Records Investigations. With the increase in background investigations as an employment screening tool, this presentation is very timely.

We are very fortunate to have as our speaker Johnny Lee, Executive Director of Peace at Work, a non-profit organization

of personal support, the victim often considers anyone who shows concern and caring a saving grace. Denying the situation at this point, especially to herself, is harder to do, so she might be ready to talk.

Set a time and location that is discreet and private. Whether it is in the manager's office, a conference room, or in the employee's workplace, the essential element is to maintain and assure confidentiality.

The subject itself is deeply personal. Only one person should broach the subject, even if a management team has decided that something needs to be done. In the best circumstances, it will be a supervisor or staff person who has developed a rapport with the potential victim, who can more easily discuss this highly embarrassing subject. I have listened to numerous reports of panel-type discussions that seemed like investigations—only the spotlight was missing from the interrogation! Such encounters only discourage victims from opening up.

Once you both settle down in a private place, get straight to the point. Do not ask if the individual is being abused. It will surprise her that someone else has noticed what she has tried very hard to conceal and make her feel ashamed. It will feel as if her problem is being thrown in her face. Her initial response is likely to be that she will try to deny that she is in this situation.

This denial may also be self-denial; the individual might not consider it abuse or think it is serious. Battered people tend to minimize the abuse; they know about shelters and the epidemic of family violence, but they honestly don't think the label applies to their situation. A woman's cultural or personal upbringing may lead her to believe that it is normal to be dominated like this. Consider the way you phrase your questions: If you ask her if she has been hit by her partner, if she is completely controlled by him, and if she is deathly afraid, she will probably answer yes to all three questions. Quite often, victims do not realize their role and status until they are out of the relationship, but they can answer a question about what happened and how they feel.

Describe the observations that warranted the concern. Without being too critical or pointing out things that embarrass the victim, detail the behaviors or indications that led to the request to meet. Be sure you emphasize that you will keep the matter confidential. You might have to notify appropriate personnel if there is a danger to the workplace, but it is important to reassure the employee-victim that whatever she tells you will not become water-cooler gossip.

It is very important to explain *why* you are inquiring into their situation. Let the individual know that you are concerned and want to help. If the intention is sincere and there is a genuine concern, the victim will be aware of the purpose of the discussion and will be more likely to open up. If a supervisor has to initially bring up the subject because of performance, explain that it is more than that. Don't get too personal and don't look like you're meddling in her business, but be sure that the person who has the discussion with the employee also expresses a desire to help with the crisis. The manager must do this as well.

Listed below are some ways to start the discussion:

- ▲ *"I am not trying to pry into your business. I am just concerned ..."*
- ▲ *"Something tells me that everything is not all right with you—that you may need some help ..."*
- ▲ *"I really hope I am wrong, but I have the feeling that you might be scared or in danger ..."*
- ▲ *"I am worried about you. Are you being hurt or threatened by anyone?"*
- ▲ *"Help me understand what is going on here. You usually do such a great job, but lately there have been some things I couldn't help but notice ..."*
- ▲ *"I will come right to the point. Do you feel safe at home?"*

Resistance

The individual will know just what you are talking about, even before you go into the details of what you have observed. Even when they have been trying to hide the evidence of the abuse, victims are relieved when someone finally asks what is going on. It is a window out of the isolation and the burden that they bear in solitude. The vast majority of the time, they will know where you are going with this discussion and what you are referring to.

If the person approaching the victim has been there or knows someone who has, he or she will have direct knowledge of what domestic violence is, and this empathy will truly help reduce feelings of isolation or shame. It can help establish a confidential link or connection. One person's disclosure might encourage the other's, but it must be sincere and come from a real understanding. Never say, *"I understand what you are going through ..."* unless you actually *do.*

Sometimes victims deny that there has been abuse. Don't be too quick to second-guess yourself. It is more likely that the victim is not prepared at this moment to discuss the matter (or even confront the reality to themselves). She might be embarrassed or is afraid to talk about it at any length, so don't pursue the subject. This would truly be intrusive, and might even antagonize her. Simply tell her that support can be given, and offer the referral that is available. If job performance is an issue, stay on that subject and explain what expectations there are and what means the organization has to help the individual meet those standards.

Do not be discouraged at your first meeting. It has not been a wasted effort, because most likely, the individual will remember the referral information and appreciate the fact that someone tried to reach out to them. If a time comes when she is ready to seek help or the situation becomes so terrible that she wants out, she will remember your attempt to discuss the matter and will likely seek you out again. On that note, it is important to leave that door open. Even if there is a flat denial, let her know that you will always be available, and that the company will provide support.

If the victim does start to disclose, the most helpful thing you can do is listen. Do not speak or interrupt. Allow for silence. Victims of abuse very often have no one to talk to about it, and there is a tremendous amount of shame in admitting to their role in the abuse. Let us be clear here: You are a supervisor or a manager; *you are not a counselor.* There is no need to spend hours learning all the details of the abuse or how it has affected the employee. Professionals who are trained and experienced in this field should handle these delicate conversations.

That said, it is important to believe the story that this person is telling you. There is much fear and shame in explaining their story; the victim will quickly stop talking if she feels that you do not believe her. Listen without judgment, and pay attention.

Here are a couple of tips that can help you handle this situation:

- ▲ Show that you are listening by rephrasing back to the victim only the main points that have been made.
- ▲ Identify any emotions or feelings you believe she is experiencing. For example, if the victim refers to her children, say that you know she must be worried about them and how the situation is affecting them.
- ▲ If the individual talks about the physical abuse and the threats, think of how you would feel if you were in her shoes: Don't express how scary and terrifying it must be—this will just acknowledge how serious and frightening the abuse is.
- ▲ Instead of parroting back what was said, condense it to emphasize the victim's main concerns.
- ▲ Tell her that you recognize the courage it takes to even talk about the abuse.
- ▲ Show your respect; this will encourage the individual to move forward and seek help.

However handled, no two encounters will be the same—there will be different reactions and responses. The basic principles are the same, however: be sincerely concerned and be willing to help. This will ensure a positive interchange.

Pitfalls

There are two very common and grave mistakes that people often make when talking to victims: Asking them why they simply don't leave, or pushing them to leave immediately or take other critical measures. Do not feel guilty if either of these impulses wells up inside you while you are talking with the victim: Even seasoned veterans in the victim-advocacy field feel the compulsion to ask these questions, especially when children are involved. It is natural to want to get the individual away from the abuse or to put him in jail, but resist the urge to make these comments or suggestions, because it is counter-productive and risky.

If you are trying to help an employee who is being abused, you must do everything you can NOT to make them feel that they are wrong to stay (which asking *why* suggests). Not only is the victim being criticized and beaten, but now she feels that she is at fault for being in the situation. The truth is that victims ask themselves why they stay in the relationship after every act of abuse, and the answer is that they believe the abuser will kill them if they leave. Advocates and law enforcement professionals know all too well that a victim's chance of being killed greatly increases once she leaves the abuser. Pushing her to leave or press charges or get a restraining order might endanger her life.

If you feel a very personal sense of protection and concern for the employee-victim or co-worker, you will want to offer financial support or a place to stay, and you might offer to go with them to the police station or even confront the abuser. Be careful: This might put you both in mortal danger. Domestic violence is about control, and if that control is threatened, the abuser might feel that a higher degree of violence is needed to re-establish dominance. This is why you *don't* want to encourage a victim to leave before she has the proper support in place and a plan.

This is not to suggest that staying and continuing to be victimized is best—the victim should leave when she is ready and prepared and it is safe. Pressure the victim to leave before she is personally ready to end the relationship, and she will most certainly end up going back to him. It truly needs to be her decision. The victim is more likely to remain independent and is less likely to return if she is adequately prepared. Couples who have lived together for many years have financial, personal, and tangible entanglements that will take some time to work out. If there are young children, this will complicate matters drastically. Taking the time to prepare, gathering the documents and materials, and putting affairs in order will make this extremely difficult transition much easier.

Finally (and most importantly), there has to be a safety plan to help prevent deadly retribution. Make a referral to proper authorities, and try to provide resources that can help assess the risk and determine the safest course of action. Chapter 7 will explore this subject in more detail.

Conclusion

It would not have taken much to approach my co-worker in that diner in Albuquerque. I know now that skirting the issue and ignoring such glaring signs of abuse is much harder than expressing concern. The hardest step is the first one: making the decision to talk and actually start the conversation. Once the words start flowing, the gravity of the situation takes over. However uncomfortable it is to start a conversation like that, it is *nothing* compared to the nightmare that victims encounter at home. Just listening without judgment is extremely beneficial, but be ready to describe what support and services are available. This will give real meaning and purpose to the discussion, and provide a glimmer of hope to a scared and traumatized victim who thought there was no way out.

Chapter 7

Management Support

For one software company located in the Research Triangle Park area of North Carolina, the harassment and abuse one employee endured was impossible to ignore—the abuser was clearly determined to get Colleen G. fired. After she left him for fear of her own and her children's safety, he used the telephone as his instrument to try to ruin her life at work. When he could not reach her directly, he left messages on the main line for other employees to hear—obscene, degrading, and vulgar descriptions that were purposely devised to upset and embarrass the victim. Colleen's abuser hoped to shame her into quitting her job, but she needed to keep it to provide a home and food for her two children. Realizing that a couple of calls were not enough, the guy started to call more frequently. Answering the phones was one of her responsibilities at the time, and every time they rang, she tensed. She dreaded picking up the phone, and this affected her ability to work. The calls increased to an unbelievable frequency. In perhaps one of the worst incidents, he called to harass and threaten her 600 times in a single workday, according to the company phone records. This disruption not only affected Colleen, but also the entire company because the abuser had the audacity to call on the company's 800 line! Only through the commendable and tenacious efforts of the business owner was the staff able to protect the victim from receiving those calls and stop the disruptive phone calls altogether. With her company's continued support, Colleen was able to overcome her abuser's attempts to ruin her life and continue on with her career. The loyalty she expressed so fervently in words and through hard work won Colleen a promotion with that company.

From the video *The Workplace Responds—*
Domestic Violence in the Workplace,
Produced by the Office of Victims of Crimes and the Family
Violence Prevention Fund
(see the Organizational Resources section in the Appendix)

Once the warning signs have been confirmed and the employee or co-worker has talked about what she or he has been going through, police, attorneys, and counselors will probably have to become involved. What can an employer do to help the victim regain their self-esteem, their skills, and their ability? Do human resources personnel have to have advanced training in the dynamics of domestic violence? How involved should a supervisor become in this very personal and complicated matter?

The answer is relatively simple and straightforward: Show them where they can get help. Allow victims the opportunity to work with the agencies and services that will address their predicament. Make a few adjustments to their personnel files. These simple tasks will probably not be time- or resource-consuming, but they can make a world of difference. A checklist of these measures is available in the Appendix.

Personal Involvement

Before we get into the subject of agency referrals, we need to talk about becoming personally involved. In many small businesses, employees and owners have developed deep, valued friendships with one another. In some, employees are considered part of the family.

The value of an employer's compassionate concern and care cannot be overestimated. The victim has social contact and interpersonal relationships that make them feel appreciated for their worth, boosting their morale and determination to eventually leave. This personal encouragement is crucial, but consider carefully how you should help.

Your first thought should be about safety. How risky is it if employers and co-workers step in (especially if the victim stays at a co-worker's home)? If the victim needs to escape because her life is in danger, wherever she stays might end up being a crime scene. A persistent abuser can easily find out where she is. Staff members at shelters for battered women are aware of this threat and have developed good safety plans. Whatever supportive actions you take, be sure the safety of all those involved has been considered first.

A quick note about employer bravado: Paternal supervisors or managers sometimes think they can intimidate the abuser. Batterers tend to consider this a challenge. It can also fuel their jealous nature. The intent to protect is admirable and important, but it is no substitute for professional expertise. Professional intervention for specific issues (law enforcement, victim-advocates, etc.) is crucial. Such professionals have experience, protocol, and training and will cover points and considerations that good intentions miss. The support of employers and co-workers is extremely important; just be sure that safety comes first, and let the professionals help.

Referrals

A supervisor might be reluctant to approach an individual because he or she does not want to be too involved. Supervisors are not counselors, and should not hear all the dramatic details of the abuse. Always let the professionals provide crisis counseling and advice. Supervisors, employers, and co-workers just need to know where to refer a victim for counseling, legal help, and safety planning. The victim should be encouraged to contact a professional or agency whose whole focus is on assisting the victims of domestic abuse. The company's Employee Assistance Plan manager and domestic violence organizations provide confidential and pivotal support.

EMPLOYEE ASSISTANCE PROGRAMS

The primary purpose of Employee Assistance Programs (EAP) is to help employees return to a fully functioning and productive status at work. The professionals are skilled generalists who can handle issues such as substance abuse, behavioral problems, and marital difficulties. It is the specialists who understand a specific issue best. EAP professionals (in-house or out-sourced) are usually familiar with issues related to domestic violence, and should have the knowledge, training, and experience to sensitively discuss the problem with the employee. They will also have the necessary contacts in the community. EAP professionals must be involved in the development of a company's violence prevention and response program. If they are contracted, they are likely to have helped other organizations with such policies and programs.

While individual policies and programs vary widely, most EAPs follow a similar format. Employees rarely need to get approval from a supervisor to get EAP help. The meetings are confidential, free, and designed to help the client identify what they need and then to find people who can address their concerns. The victim might be referred to a counselor who will address the emotional and psychological impact of the abuse, but the local domestic-violence agency or organization can also offer licensed crisis counselors (and much more). Supervisors should realize that what goes on in the session between the EAP professional and the employee is strictly confidential. However, it is best to include such professionals in threat-management meetings to help determine the level of risk to the workplace, and to decide how to support the victim. Without revealing the details of their discussion, the EAP professional might be obligated to report what they believe is likely to happen (i.e., a violent act).

DOMESTIC VIOLENCE SERVICE PROVIDERS

The true experts in the field of domestic violence are the advocates whose mission is to help victims create a new life of safety and well-being, free from abuse and control. These programs have grown in recognition, funding, and professionalism, but many smaller communities have only grass-roots operations. These non-profit organizations work closely with police, the courts, and community advocacy organizations. Individuals responsible for handling domestic violence problems in the workplace must be familiar with the services available locally, even if the nearest organization is a few hours away.

What happens when a domestic-violence organization steps in? First, an initial assessment is done to determine a victim's level of danger. A crisis counselor will carefully and sensitively evaluate the victim's current situation to determine what the abuser is capable of doing (and the likelihood that the abuser will carry out such an act). If the victim is thinking of leaving the abuser, the primary focus will be on how to do it safely, with the greatest chance of success. The counselor can then develop a plan with the victim to reduce the chance of violence, should she choose to remain with her partner. She will be taught how to remain safe when the abuser becomes enraged or abusive, how to prepare to leave, and where to go if she does leave her abuser. Putting key items like legal papers, money, spare clothes, and an extra set of keys in a safe, discreet place for when she needs them and deciding where to go are both part of the plan. A hotel room, a relative, or the domestic violence shelter are options that should be weighed ahead of time.

These agencies also provide safe houses or shelters in order to protect the victim from further abuse or homicide. These inconspicuous locations hide a woman (and her children) from an abuser for a short period of time. Shelters for male victims are relatively scarce or non-existant at this time. Hundreds of women across the country are protected in shelters each day, and for some who have no place to go or who are in fear for their lives, a shelter is their only option. These are no ramshackle dorms; they are usually nondescript houses in family neighborhoods, where each family can have its own room. Unfortunately, domestic violence is becoming more of a problem and these facilities are often filled to capacity. Most agencies will work together to help place a victim (even in another community, if a victim believes that the abuser knows where the shelter is located). It is important to note here that while a victim is safe at a shelter, she will probably need a job so that she can save enough money for a permanent place to live.

Advocacy organizations can provide crisis counseling and longer-term counseling with a licensed therapist. Many advocates are themselves survivors who can truly empathize and understand the feelings and concerns of the victim, while still maintaining an objective and professional perspective. This understanding can be an oasis for victims who feel isolated, embarrassed, and ashamed.

Support groups are extremely beneficial. They offer encouragement and the realization that the abuse is not the victim's fault. Sharing with others who understand how a victim feels and who have also endured increases a woman's self-esteem and confidence that she too can create a life free from abuse. Many programs have counterpart groups for the children (who have likely witnessed some of the abuse).

Although advocacy organizations cannot provide legal counsel, they can often help with tasks associated with civil and criminal charges, such as filling out paperwork for a restraining order, explaining what will happen in court, and even sitting through the tedious and embarrassing court hearings. Such agencies also work closely with non-profit, legal aid organizations that have attorneys on staff for more in-depth legal help.

As you can see, such agencies step in to handle the basics, but they often do quite a bit more in terms of prevention. Community outreach and awareness campaigns help the public understand how drastic and common the issue is and where people can go for help. Raising community awareness alone is a considerable achievement. The ways that a company or organization can support these efforts (to the benefit of the company), the shelter, and the communities in which they exist will be discussed in a later chapter.

CORPORATE AND SHELTER PARTNERSHIPS

Advocates and counselors cannot divulge what is said during sessions with victims or abusers or the details about a specific case, but they can help businesses in a variety of ways.

Domestic-violence professionals can help with policy development and training, but one of the most-important functions is to help HR professionals and supervisors understand what a victim is going through and what challenges they face. An advocate's primary concern is the safety and well-being of the victim; most likely, the advocate will persuade an employer to offer the most support and protection to the victim employee. Security professionals and attorneys will recommend the best ways to protect the workplace and its interests. An advocate can provide a professional and rational perspective on the victim's needs, perhaps when the victim herself is not able to do so. It is important to collaborate with such agencies to get a broader and more comprehensive picture of the situation. Invite a representative from the local domestic violence service provider to a meeting to help with the broader assessment of the situation and make a thorough determination of applicable action steps.

A referral source for state and local resources can be found in the Appendix. Employers should become familiar with local community resources (especially through support and active participation). The experience itself will be rewarding.

Administrative Support

If you are at work right now, imagine not being able to go home today. If you are at home, imagine having to move *right now*. Think of what it would be like to have all your assets and personal items taken from you or unavailable. You might be able to find a new place to live and establish yourself by changing your mailing address and physically moving any available personal property, but what about having to deal with the court systems? Many people have received a court summons because they ignored a few motor vehicle citations, but imagine having to press serious criminal charges or file a civil suit against an adversary who doesn't mind dragging the case out—and intentionally tries to waste your time. It usually takes at least two days to get a domestic violence restraining order. Criminal court hearings are often postponed or continued with rarely any notification beforehand. Now consider medical or counseling appointments. Everyone knows the boredom and monotony of waiting to see a doctor, only to learn that you have to schedule return visits or get referrals for other specialists. Throw in crisis counseling sessions at the shelter, meetings with police officers who are investigating the case, the pressing need to change locks on doors, get another vehicle, and register the kids at new schools and you will begin to comprehend the challenges that victims face in order to successfully leave a domestic violence situation.

Allowing for Time Off

Obviously, one clear and simple action you can do as the employer is to allow a victim some time off. She has probably already used all of her sick leave and vacation time. Even if she has some days left, she can't give you much advanced notice for her absence. Disrupting other workers' scheduled leave and leaving you short-staffed are certainly problems, but remember that a victim of domestic violence can't plan for such emergencies. You can help by arranging innovative and alternative work schedules and work duties, however. Flexing the schedule or allowing a victim to take extra shifts at a later date are ways to help her or him take the time to manage the crisis without hampering your production. Making such allowances can be rewarding: You will get an employee who is even more dedicated to their company and who will no doubt improve her performance out of loyalty and to re-establish her own sense of self-worth.

In some cases, just a few days will be necessary, but some victims will need to take several weeks off. Many survivors have described their bosses as "walking on water" for simply saying to them, *"Go and do what you need to do. Your job will be waiting for you when you get back."* In these cases, victims were given the time to manage their affairs, and went to excel in their companies. Unburdened by the abuse and revitalized by their new look on life, they were enthusiastic about their work and full of appreciation for their companies. This rubbed off on other workers.

The Family Medical Leave Act allows employees in most companies to take up to 30 days off without fear of losing their jobs, provided there is a medical need in the immediate family. Domestic abuse is a violent and overwhelming threat to women. Violence and other forms of abuse cause serious emotional suffering; notes and reports from psychologists, psychiatrists, and other mental health professionals constitute most of the paperwork necessary for a temporary leave of absence based on psychological trauma. Obviously, it is much more beneficial for everyone if a company offers this option right away, instead of reluctantly allowing the leave after a victim gathers the medical notes and even an attorney in order to press compliance with this federal employment mandate.

Ease in Workload

If the employee works throughout the ordeal or returns to work after taking time off, she or he might not perform optimally. (This is especially true while they are in the midst of abuse.) Impartial treatment of all employees makes good business practice, but it is just as important to understand what your employees are going through. Your business success and even survival is tied to employee performance; look comprehensively at the employee's past performance, growth potential, and general value to the company and see if you can relax these duties during especially trying times. Again, with the guidance of a supervisor, a victim can reverse poor performance and regain the ability to perform to everyone's satisfaction (and even surprise).

Employee Records

One step employers often overlook in their haste to cover work-loads and assess physical security is update the employee's records. This process takes just a few minutes, but it is a crucial part of safety planning, especially if there is a violent scene at work. The name and phone numbers of every contact person should be reviewed by HR; unfortunately, the person who is listed at the time of hire is often the person now doing the victimizing. You must ask the victim for the name of someone they can trust in the event of an emergency. Naturally, the employee-victim should tell this contact person what they are going through and advise them of their role should an emergency occur.

PERSONAL CONTACT INFORMATION

If the victim has moved because she fears for her life, you must have a current phone and address, as well as the name of someone to contact. If the victim is staying in a shelter, the domestic violence agency will not give out the exact location of the house, but can provide a contact number. During the crisis period, it is not unusual for the victim to be moving from one temporary living arrangement to another (hotels, family, friends). A cell phone can be especially useful in these cases.

It is absolutely critical that you keep all contact information in the strictest confidence. A stalking abuser will go to great lengths to learn the whereabouts of his victim, including posing as an investigator or government official; some will even attempt burglary. Any attempt by anyone not working directly with the victim to obtain information about the victim must be considered suspect.

BENEFICIARY INFORMATION

Also review the beneficiary information. If the relationship is over (at least in the eyes of the victim), the abuser's name can be removed at the employee's request from any health, dental, or life insurance plans. The HR department should be able to find the easiest way to do this (i.e., switching plans from "family" plan to "individual," or "employee and children"). The abuser losing these benefits will be notified of the change by the respective insurance carriers and might be given the option to continue coverage on his own. Some divorce or separation agreements stipulate that the employee continue including the separated spouse in the policy, but this is not an immediate matter, and can be addressed later.

More importantly, it is vital to immediately remove the abuser's name as a survivor beneficiary. Retirement pension plans, 401-K plans, and life insurance policies should be changed to reflect a different recipient of benefits should the employee die. (Naturally, if the abuser is convicted of murdering or otherwise causing the death of the employee, the benefit will not be given to them anyway.) If it is a random accidental death or death from something unrelated to the abuse, it would be a shame if the person who terrorized and traumatized a victim during her life is awarded life insurance money after she dies, just because someone overlooked this simple step.

Equally outrageous is the possibility that the victim will die suspiciously and no one will be able to prove that the abuser had a hand in it. A tragically infamous case illustrates this point. In 1998, Mark Barton was found responsible for the senseless murder of 12 people. Along with bludgeoning to death his wife and two children, he killed nine employees in two separate brokerage firms in Atlanta, Georgia. Interestingly, a few years prior to the murders, he collected over $300,000 in survivor insurance benefits because his ex-wife was stabbed to death, along with her mother. FBI profilers, the District Attorney, and others familiar with the case knew that Barton was the one who killed the two women in an RV park, but without enough clear evidence, it was impossible to indict Barton. One of the two life insurance companies holding a policy on his wife tried to block Barton's court claim for benefits. They had good reason: the large life insurance policy was taken out just a few months before she was killed. A settlement was reached, and Barton got away with not only the murders, but also a large amount of money because he was the beneficiary on both policies. This travesty of justice can be averted in a few short minutes by preparing the required change forms and getting the employee-victim's signature.

Direct Deposits

As we explained in previous chapters, controlling the money is one way that abusers maintain dominance over a victim. If their partner works, she is forced to hand over her pay on a regular basis. Economic flexibility and income is a key factor in being able to leave the abuser, but simple changes can be made through the company's payroll system. If a check is currently mailed to the home where the abuser lives, she can have it sent to the home of a friend, a post office box, etc. A better arrangement is to set up direct deposit so that the paycheck goes directly from the company into a checking or savings account that only she controls. (A joint checking account that the abuser has access to can easily and legally be drained, which will frustrate the victim's attempts to live apart.) It is the victim's responsibility to open or change a bank account, but management can help by making sure that the first paycheck gets into this account as soon as possible. Small administrative steps can help a victim immeasurably.

Understanding

Understanding all the complexities from the perspective of the victim is the easiest and most supportive way to help, but it's sometimes the most difficult. Victims are in emotional and physical turmoil, but the simple act of showing real empathy will help them the most. Just be sure you don't question the victim about why she got into such a relationship or why she stays.

No matter how or why you ask such questions, it won't help the victim. Being able to open up to a trustworthy and understanding person can provide the greatest relief. Just listen. You don't have to understand the reasons or the issues that surround the relationship, but you will surely be able to relate to feelings of confusion, fear, and anxiety. If you offer respect and encouragement and rally when they take small steps toward independence, you will help reduce their feelings of isolation and fear. In case after case where an employer has supported an employee-victim, victims say that it was the *compassion* and *understanding* that they appreciated the most. Granting days off, making changes in your personnel files, and providing security are important steps, but it is your human caring that produces steadfast loyalty on the part of the employee-victim, but also from co-workers who witness such acts of kindness.

Conclusion

Some employers will be reluctant to show support out of concern that this will disrupt their "professional and objective" work environment. The reality, however, is that employees and employers spend much of their waking lives with one another. The decision to work for a specific company is very often based not on compensation or title alone, but also on the environment and culture of the workplace. The responsibilities and duties of supervisors and employers will never be as important as living the basic values of humanity. Employers and managers can do much to help a victim move on, but the actions described in this chapter are crucial to ensure their safety and the safety of your entire workforce.

Chapter 8

Security Issues

Making the entire workplace more secure is a critical part of protecting your employees from the escalating effects of domestic abuse. Implementing security measures also eases workers' fears and concerns. Rumors will spread, no matter how effective you are at keeping things confidential, and people will start to get scared. Let the staff know that you are aware of the problem and are taking action to protect them. This will instill a greater sense of loyalty, because they will see that you are more interested in keeping them from harm than in protecting your tangible assets.

This chapter is all about how to create a more secure workplace. Let's start with what can happen in the extreme:

Violence rarely comes without warning or pre-indication. In Nashville, Tennessee, Thomas Edgar Harrison continued his path of violence and brutality to tragic end. An employee at a video production rental store had been dating Harrison for several years, much of the time in fear of his behavior. When she called off the relationship in February of 2003, he had no intention of letting her go. On June 3rd, he kidnapped and held the woman against her will for five hours, raping her and threatening suicide. She miraculously was able to escape, and Harrison was arrested. This looked like the end of a horrible ordeal, but Harrison was soon released on $90,000 bail. There were serious criminal charges pending against him, but also a restraining order. Harrison didn't care: On August 29th, three months later, he came to see his ex-girlfriend at work, using a false name. He was denied access and was escorted out the door. That's when he snapped, pulling out a gun and sending panic throughout the workplace. Some employees fled, while others barricaded themselves inside their offices. Several workers risked their own lives to warn their co-workers of the danger. Greg Griffith, one of the owners, suffered the worst as he tried to protect his staff. He confronted the gunman and was ruthlessly shot and killed. Another employee managed to get the shotgun away from Harrison and throw it over a fence. Unfortunately, Harrison had a pistol also. After a prolonged standoff with the emergency response team, authorities stormed in and found Harrison inside a locked bathroom, dead from a self-inflicted gunshot wound to the head. While this implies no blame on the part of the company, it is evident from the man's recent violent and reckless behavior that he was clearly and lethally dangerous.

What would you do in this situation?

Let us look at what happened right after Thomas Harrison was released on bail. When the company saw what he was capable of doing, what measures should they have put in place? The real key is knowing what the individual is willing to do and what resources he had available to carry it out. What information-gathering and processing protocol would *you* follow to determine the level of threat? Despite the suddenness of the assault and the degree of lethality, there were warning signs that should have been picked up on and interpreted. The company also should have instituted security measures to protect the workplace and the people who gathered there.

Let's say one of your employees is being battered and verbally abused by the man she lives with. She tells her supervisor that she is certain that he is coming after her, and that he will kill her wherever he finds her. Her co-workers are showing signs of anxiety, and people are on edge and starting to feel afraid. Your teammates have genuine concerns, based on the evidence that they have uncovered during their investigation. What can a company do to protect the victim, its workforce, its customers, and the company as a whole? The situation is not as hopeless as it sounds. There are steps that can reduce the vulnerability. Professionals in the security business refer to those steps as *target hardening*.

There are two factors involved in every crime: There is the motive of the criminal, which in this case is to harm the victim and perhaps any bystanders. Then, there is an opportunity to commit the crime. Management can't do much about the motive, but if the perpetrator is an employee, management does have control over what services are available and how discipline is delivered. If you provide the potentially violent person with dignity and respect in all dealings, you reduce the level of resentment and possible retaliation.

Management can influence the second factor: the possibility that the abuser will do something violent. The security precautions listed in this chapter cannot be an absolute guarantee of safety, because even the most extreme of measures is not infallible.

This section will address the most pressing issue of which security measures are appropriate, based on the level of risk as determined by the threat assessment or management team. We will discuss general preventative measures to reduce the vulnerabilities of the business, as well as specific guidelines you can establish to protect the victim, her or his co-workers, management, and clients. A checklist is included in the Appendix that lists security measures that should be implemented.

Preliminary Note on Workplace Violence

The threat of violence in the workplace is a serious concern for every responsible business owner. Family or domestic abuse can be incorporated as a sub-topic into any organized violence-prevention program. Just be sure you have some protocol to handle workplace violence: Personnel policies, staff training, a reporting method, and a threat management system are all elements to incorporate in a comprehensive plan. We will describe how to set up a threat-management team, although it is not the purpose of this book to describe how to develop a workplace violence program. Consultants are available to help you do that quite effectively. It is, however, crucial that you put such a program in place immediately.

Assess Your Vulnerabilities

FACILITY RISK ASSESSMENT

Do not wait until a threat is identified to assess the company's risk *or* its ability to manage a crisis. You must take the time to thoroughly evaluate your vulnerability to any kind of criminal activity, including violence. If an abuser enters the place where his partner works and harms people or damages property, the company might feel an immediate need to increase physical security, but it will be too late to do the most important things. It is important to any company's success to ensure the safety of the facility, and it is its responsibility. It should take advance measures that help prevent any crime from occurring— robberies, sexual assaults, vandalism, and so on.

The study of security measures is known as "Crime Prevention through Environmental Design" or CPTED. A combination of physical adaptations will make it more difficult for a perpetrator to reach his or her target: additional lighting on the inside and more importantly on the outside of the facility; gates and barriers that act as effective obstacles to any intrusion; more-secure windows and doors with locking mechanisms; and even the layout of the actual facility are all crucial for safety. Almost every facility will have areas designated only for visitors and customers. Be sure you have defined these areas and restrict access to them. Surveillance does nothing to physically stop a perpetrator from committing a crime, but closed-circuit cameras can be a deterrent and provide hard evidence in the event of a trial. Special attention should be paid to the parking lot, as it is one of the most vulnerable places on company grounds. Many victims of abuse have been killed in the company parking areas.

Obviously, these are just the basics. Security is an entire industry. To assess your business's weaknesses, consider hiring a security consultant to make recommendations, and be sure to develop a relationship with local police. Its crime prevention unit can also help you conduct a facility risk assessment (perhaps as a community service).

The cost of a security consultant's services and the resulting implementation of any recommendations will affect the management's decision as to the extent of protection. A company's vulnerabilities, opportunities to collaborate with surrounding businesses (whether or not the company owns the property), and customer accessibility are all points that also must be weighed.

PROCEDURE RISK ASSESSMENT

We've taken a brief look at the risks to the physical structure and the use of technology. No matter how much money you spend or how advanced your security equipment is, everything you do can be rendered useless by human error. Remember that actual habits and work practices create the safety risks: Be sure you carefully review staffing, identification protocol, and other issues of work behavior. What you find in terms of risk will be illuminating.

Are your people required to wear ID badges? Do you require all visitors to sign in and wear identification? Have you designated certain doorways for certain uses? These are all operational procedures that help maintain security in many institutions. However, it is the lax enforcement of these things that makes the measures obsolete: While it might seem useless for long-term employees in a small work environment to wear ID tags (since everyone knows each other), the point is to be able to tell who doesn't belong there if there is an unfamiliar face. In relaxed and family-friendly environments, it is very common for spouses to visit employees at their workstation, especially around lunch or break times. Frequent visitors who are not employees have the same unlimited access to areas prohibited to the public, increasing the risk of violent confrontation.

The back door of a facility is the Achilles heel, especially when the front-door personnel are warned *not* to let an abuser in due to identified risk for violent behavior. The perpetrator who has been a frequent visitor meets someone he knows at the back entrance (perhaps they shared a drink at the last company party). The employee, not aware that this individual is banned from the facility, allows the abuser to piggy-back or follow behind as he or she enters an otherwise secure door requiring an ID card-swipe or key. Many doors have keypad entries that require a code to unlock the portal. However, if you take a survey of spouses of employees to see who knows the company's entry codes, you will be shocked. Developing or implementing security procedures is all well and good, but employee behavior can undermine these prevention efforts.

Many companies have strict no-visitation policies while employees are working. In certain industries, this measure is valid and necessary, but depending on the culture of the company and the work environment of the office or workspace, this can be inconvenient and frustrating for the employees. As with all security measures, weigh the level of convenience against the safety of the business. Try sending strong and persistent reminders to all employees to follow the guidelines. Every visitor, no matter how familiar and innocuous, should be required to sign in at the front door.

There are two dangerous working practices that will jeopardize the safety of a victim. Working with the public and handling cash significantly increases the chances of a robbery, but sales clerks working alone are also solitary and easy targets. Having a job that requires an individual to work alone is, by far, the riskiest job for a victim if their workplace is a public one (retail sales clerks, cashiers, carriers, etc.). Those who must travel, especially to known locations or on a predictable route, are possibly the most vulnerable because they are often alone and they are away from the facility. In one domestic violence case, the victim was an employee of an educational institution, and her job was to transport children on field trips. Her ex-husband had made repeated threats that had to be considered valid, given the history of aggravated abuse she had experienced throughout her relationship with him. She was vulnerable because she was an easy target from the parking lot to anywhere along the travel route, but the safety of the children was also being jeopardized. What if there was a confrontation in front of them? Even worse, what if a child was assaulted? The obvious first step was to remove this woman from these duties.

Roles and Responsibilities

THREAT MANAGEMENT TEAM

Before there is an incident, immediately set up a team of people responsible for developing and ensuring proper implementation of any policies regarding workplace violence. This group's responsibility is likely to be to assess and address any actual threat. In smaller companies, one or two selected employees and/or the business owner can be put in charge of all management decisions and actions related to the threat. In mid- to large-size companies, the team can be made up of people who handle different functions of the organization. The advantage of having several people on the team is that rather than having just one person considering all the facets of such a vital safety issue, you have several.

Which areas of the company should be represented on your threat-management team? Representatives from a variety of departments and expertise should participate, including human resources, legal counsel, security, and line supervisors. If you do not have such diversity in your organization, seek help from outside agencies such as law enforcement. It is this team's responsibility to determine how severe a specific threat is, what appropriate action should and will be taken, and what other resources can be acquired to assure safety. Have the team meet regularly to establish relationships, determine expectations, and practice going through the procedures before any actual crisis erupts.

Again, it is not within the scope of this book to outline complete procedures for threat-assessment. That said, there are certain characteristics of domestic-violence situations that warrant more-stringent security measures. Ask yourself these questions:

- ▲ Has the abuser seriously assaulted the employee-victim, or anyone else? Did any assault call for medical treatment? Did any of these assaults involve the use of a weapon?
- ▲ Does the victim believe that the abuser will try to kill her?
- ▲ Does the abuser have familiarity with or access to firearms?
- ▲ Has the abuser made direct or veiled threats to kill or seriously harm the victim? Has he threatened to kill himself?
- ▲ Is this person fanatically obsessed with the victim? Does the abuser feel that he or she "owns" the victim and/or cannot live without her?
- ▲ Has the abuser given up on all aspects of his life? Does he show a lack of interest in work, home, family, financial concerns, or other personal matters?
- ▲ Has the abuser hurt or killed any of the victim's pets?
- ▲ Does the abuser have substance abuse issues?

While the absence of these indicators does not imply complete safety, neither do all of the factors guarantee that there will be a violent and possibly fatal assault. They are just pre-indicators that are more common in cases where violence has occurred.

DEVELOP A LIAISON WITH THE LOCAL LAW ENFORCEMENT AGENCY

The team must contact the local police department long before there is any actual need to address a specific threat. Developing a relationship with local police is a primary step: They can be instrumental should there be an investigation, and having a good working relationship is simply good business practice.

Once a threat has been determined, most police departments have divisions that work directly with community crime prevention—perhaps a community resource officer, or even an entire crime-prevention unit whose role it is to work with the citizens to identify crime risks and help prevent an incident. A growing number of agencies have trained personnel in domestic violence issues. Police can help with security, but they are also sources of a wealth of information and general expertise in dealing with extremely volatile crises.

Try to get one police officer to serve as your liaison—an officer who will be familiar with any specific threat should it escalate. Invite the officer to the workplace so that he or she can get to know the actual layout of the facility and grounds and meet the key players. Explain what the team has done so far and ask for additional suggestions.

Once you have a designated emergency response official who is familiar with the situation should the worst occur, you will no longer have to worry about someone responding to an emergency. The informed officer can work with the responding units to provide critical details, and might even be the first to respond. Be sure to provide this person and the department with the schematics or layout of the facility before there is an emergency. Having this on file is invaluable to responding officers during a shoot-out or hostage situation.

It should be noted here that law enforcement agencies vary in the resources they can make available. Not all of them will be able to provide the time and personnel if nothing has happened yet. They will have to respond to actual crimes in progress or that have been reported, so their time will be limited. Most law enforcement agencies recognize the value of working closely with the communities they serve, however. By being patient but persistent, you can improve the security of your facility by having a liaison within the local police department.

Legal Actions

The criminal and civil court system can help protect victims and their employers from their abusers. Most of these remedies are carried out each day in courtrooms throughout the country, and do not require the services of an attorney or other legal representation. They are thus readily accessible and affordable to smaller companies that do not have in-house counsel. States will vary in terms of the type and extent of domestic violence measures, but they all provide fundamental assistance.

Involving the judicial system does bring a very influential and authoritative player into the arena. Many perpetrators fearful of monetary fines, court costs, damage to their reputations and their employment, and most significantly, jail time will stop abusing once a deputy delivers a summons to court. However, there have been cases where taking out a protective order or drawing up a criminal warrant pushes the abuser over the edge, and they will seek total retribution. Every decision you make about how to handle a potential threat to the workplace must first be evaluated in terms of safety. And there must be input from the victim.

DOMESTIC VIOLENCE RESTRAINING ORDERS

A peace or protective order is a civil action that carries criminal consequences if it is violated. Only the threatened victim can request a restraining order, which prohibits the accused from coming within so many yards of the victim's home, workplace, or other necessary locations. It generally prohibits any communication, including phone calls, e-mails, letters, and electronic paging (even through third parties). Some restraining orders will give the victim temporary custody of children and possession of the home and vehicles, as well as provide other stipulations to ensure protection.

There is a federal law that bans possession of firearms by anyone who has a restraining order against them, although this law is rarely enforced on the state level. At the hearing, a victim or their representative can request to have the judge either order the defendant to relinquish their firearms to police, or have a deputy sent to the residence to confiscate known weapons. What will actually happen depends on the particular district and judge presiding over the court. The active order should also prohibit the abuser from buying firearms from any licensed gun dealer. While it is relatively easy for a tenacious person to obtain a gun from other sources, this provision, if enforced, can remove current firearms and make it difficult to get more.

Obtaining a domestic violence restraining order is a fairly simple thing. The victim/plaintiff goes to the courthouse to fill out the paperwork with the Clerk of Court, and will be able to go before a judge soon afterward (perhaps even the same day) to obtain a temporary order (sometimes known as an *ex parte*), which is usually in effect for ten days. Magistrates can issue temporary restraining orders when courts are closed. These might be good only for 24 hours: The victim will have to return to the courthouse to go before the judge. The defendant/abuser does not have to be present. According to the Federal Violence Against Women Act, there is to be no charge for this civil action, and it does not require an attorney to file. After a prescribed period of time and after the abuser has been served with the court summons, a full hearing is held with both parties to determine if the court order should be made permanent (this is a misnomer, because it is often good for only an additional year, though it can be renewed). If the order is maintained and is subsequently violated, the victim can go to the police. Violation of such orders is a criminal act that can result in possible incarceration and/or fines.

In most areas, domestic violence agencies or other victim advocates can help the victim get a restraining order. Trained and experienced representatives can help explain and fill out the paperwork, guide the victims on what to tell the judge, and sit with them through the court hearing. Even with this help, court sessions will probably take two days or more, barring any continuances and delays. The employer's support in allowing for time off for this is crucial.

Restraining orders can be written to include the workplace. If it is listed as a prohibited area, the abuser is prohibited from entering, but restraining orders also ban them from even approaching the facility within a certain distance. It can also prohibit communication with the victim, thus addressing what to do about the debilitating issue of harassing phone calls and threats at work. The company must get its own copy of the order, communicate with the contact person at the police department, and be able to readily present the document to officials, should it be necessary.

TRESPASS ORDERS

A business that is open to the public and for whom accessibility is vital to success can bar a particular individual from entering it. Whether it is a hostile ex-employee, a disgruntled client, or an employee's violent abuser, the offending individual can be served legal orders banning them from a particular location. All that is required is for the company to prove that the individual is a credible threat or nuisance to the establishment. A trespass order does not bar them from trying to communicate, so persistent phone calls and messages might still be permissible as long as they are not threatening. The process of banning someone will range from asking an officer to deliver a formal letter to holding a court hearing. Local police can explain more about this procedure.

WORKPLACE RESTRAINING ORDERS

There have been a number of new laws put into effect around the country regarding *workplace restraining orders*. In essence, an employer and/or business owner can obtain a restraining order similar to that used for individuals that prohibits the identified individual from entering, approaching, or making any contact with the protected establishment or its employees. It differs from the domestic violence restraining order in that it can be used against *any* type of threat (a loitering nuisance who disturbs customers, an ex-employee who has vowed revenge for being laid off, a client who intimidates employees with ultimatums, etc.). Although it can be applied to family violence situations, the workplace restraining order only pertains to the workplace and job activities; it cannot be extended to the victim's home life or to non-work activities. The other significant point is that it is the employer who obtains the order, not the person who is being harassed and threatened.

This option addresses several important concerns. First, it is a very clear sign of support to an employee, and can shift the "blame" off the victim because it is the employer, not the victim, who is taking the legal action. Basically, the victim can benefit from the protections that the order provides, but she or he does not have to be the one responsible for "defying" the abuser.

However, such an order can have a direct and grave consequence on the victim's life. Victims are reluctant to obtain an order for a variety of reasons, central of which is that it can enrage the abuser and propel him into violence anyway. A restraining order is just a piece of paper; the key witness in the hearing to obtain the order is often the same person who is receiving the threats. This person might be reluctant to go to court, stand next to their abuser, and testify to all the embarrassing and terrifying details in a public courtroom. Therefore, it is vital not to coerce or hold any threat of disciplinary action against an employee who does not participate in the procedure. Not only would the employer be acting as another authority mandating control over their life, but it would make the victim (and any other unknown employee-victims who are aware of it) less inclined to disclose their own threats or concerns that management needs to know.

A well-documented case study clearly illustrates what I mean. During the mid-1980s, Richard Farley, an employee of the ESL corporation, had an obsession with a co-worker named Laura Black. This was not a typical domestic violence situation in that there never was any type of social relationship between the two parties. It still had all the symptoms of stalking, harassment, and control. Even after losing his job and most material possessions, Farley continued to stalk his victim at home and at her workplace (his former workplace). After alleged continued pressure from her employer and hints that refusal could affect her potential for promotion, Laura Black applied for a restraining order, despite her concerns about how Farley would react. In the courtroom, she stated that she was reluctant to do it and was keenly aware that what she called "this piece of paper" could do very little in providing actual protection, and might even "set him off." Her intuition was right: The day before the hearing that would have made the restraining order permanent, Farley came to the job site and shot ten people, killing seven of them. Laura Black, seriously wounded, barely escaped with her life. *The Gift of Fear* by Gavin de Becker (Dell Publishing, 1997) is an excellent resource on this case.

This tragic incident has important lessons for anyone considering any type of restraining order:

1. Listen to the concerns and opinions of the victims who actually endure the abuse. Victims are experts in survival: They know what the abuser is capable of doing and how they will react to any actions.
2. A protective order is not enough to adequately protect a person or a workplace. It simply threatens the person who violates the order with a misdemeanor criminal charge and is not effective unless there is response from a law enforcement unit. Other security measures are needed to increase the safety of the victim and co-workers.

It is important to identify the vulnerabilities of this civil action, but do not let this discourage you from obtaining a workplace restraining order. It is a very good way to stop continual and interfering calls from abusers who fear judicial involvement. It also mandates police response if the abuser is spotted near a facility. I must emphasize two things about restraining orders: First, never turn to them as knee-jerk reactions, and never use them as the sole means of protection. An in-depth and comprehensive threat assessment must be made to reasonably determine the degree of risk, the abuser's likely reaction to a restraining order, and finally, what other security measures will be or should be implemented.

CIVIL SUITS

If the actions of an abuser cause any actual and monetary damages to a company's interests, the company can file a lawsuit against the abuser. Was an employee's time squandered and did their ability to function deteriorate because they were harassed? Was there actual damage to property in the form of vandalism or malicious destruction? Were customers scared away, or business profits otherwise affected that can be directly attributed to the abuser's behaviors? I have yet to discover a court case centered on this issue, but the grounds for this action are valid and these situations are quite common, so it is possible for such trials to occur. Consult the company's attorney to determine the cost of undertaking such action or whether or not it might incite a violent response and further expose the company.

CRIMINAL CHARGES

Pressing criminal charges is often the most critical and yet most serious part of any domestic violence situation. There are several issues that must be made clear right away: First and foremost, everyone involved must understand that *domestic violence is a crime*. It is not simply a problem related to family squabbles or marital problems or anger/substance abuse. It is a criminal act, just as robbing a bank, forging bad checks, and car jacking are criminal acts. It needs to be prevented because violent actions have consequences.

Next, there is the question of who the victim of the specific crime is. In general, the victim is the only one who can press charges because she or he is the victim of the crime. An officer of the law can do it, but only when there is probable cause—if, for example, there has been an assault and an officer has witnessed the injuries on a victim and files charges on the abuser. An employer cannot file assault charges against the abuser of an employee-victim.

However, perhaps the company is the victim of certain criminal actions. Did the abuser damage any company property? Trespass into non-public areas? Incessantly make harassing phone calls to a business phone? If so, the company suffering from these actions can file a police report and/or draw warrants. It is important to work with a law enforcement liaison to determine if the reason is valid and decide on next steps. In criminal cases, the state's prosecutor will handle the court trial, but it is always advisable to consult with the company's attorney as well. State laws vary widely when it comes to the more-subtle forms of criminal activity, such as stalking, trespassing, and harassment.

There are additional advantages to obtaining criminal warrants. First, the defendant might have to spend time in jail prior to the court hearing. This would certainly hamper any attempts to continue the harassment or threaten the victim. If the individual is released on bail or released bond, the defendant will be warned not to harass, threaten, or intimidate the plaintiff in any manner. The idea is to protect the witnesses or plaintiffs from the perpetrator's attempt to get the charges dropped. If the judge's warnings are ignored, a charge such as *intimidating a state's witness* can put them right back in jail under stiffer penalties. A criminal warrant is not the same as a protective order; contact is allowed between the parties, but the defendant cannot intimidate or pressure the victim to drop the charges or pressure a witness to lie. Unfortunately, other forms of coercion are common. The *"Oh baby, I am so sorry," "I promise this will never happen again,"* and *"This will ruin me"* are all common ploys, and in many cases they work. A large percentage of charges are dropped in courtrooms around the country every day—incomprehensible to many managers. Anticipate this fairly common action, and be sure to continue supporting the victim in any way you can.

Stopping the Harassment and Collecting Evidence

Before we get into security measures that physically protect the victim and the workplace, let's look at one very simple yet effective step a company can take to not only relieve the victim, but also to provide material to help prosecute the abuser. Quite often, the abuser will harass and threaten their victim through phone calls, e-mails, messages, and other forms of communication. This behavior has a debilitating effect on an employee's ability to function at work because work is constantly being interrupted, and the victim knows that her abuser is intentionally playing with her emotions. Phone calls that are made to the victim should be redirected through a screening process to determine if they are valid inquiries or just attempts by the abuser or his or her associates to reach the victim. A receptionist, security guard, or supervisor can take all calls for the victim and then forward them if they are appropriate.

The company has an opportunity here to contribute evidence should there be a court trial or police investigation: The company can provide the victim with a new e-mail address and phone extension and maintain the old one to collect any threatening messages. A direct threat, made under any circumstances, is a criminal act, and contact of any form is prohibited if there is a restraining order in place. Business-related communication can still be identified and replied to, but you should preserve any evidence of harassment. Telephone calls and e-mail messages can be traced by law enforcement professionals to the origination point, even if no name is left in the voice mail system and it appears anonymous. Abusers recklessly leave detailed, hateful messages and sometimes even identify who they are. The rashness of such behavior must be taken into consideration during a threat assessment; be sure to assess how impulsive and desperate an abuser might be if he or she is so compelled to leave self-incriminating messages despite the threat of jail time for violating a protective order. This individual might be willing to throw his or her life away in a desperate, violent act, and the company must let the police know of this concern as soon as possible.

Any tangible communication in the form of notes, letters, or packages should be handled as little as possible so as to not obscure any fingerprints. Threatening letters sent by mail can lead to further charges, but the reality is that police will probably be reluctant to lift fingerprints from a letter for just a "communication threat" or harassment charge. Such cases are frequent and numerous; police do time-consuming evidence collection only when proof of authorship is required for the most serious assaults or when it is for a homicide investigation case. One final note: Packages of any type must be handled carefully, as they can be rigged with explosives or contain toxic or biological substances. Suspicious packages should be left alone and authorities notified immediately.

Developing a Security Plan

If you do not have a security plan, it is time to develop one. Risk assessments and legal restrictions will not protect the victim and other employees if the abuser is intent on violent confrontation and is willing to die anyway. Approximately 43 percent of the violent incidents researched in a 2004 Peace@Work study involved abusers who attempted to kill themselves during the rampage. Many succeeded. This reality has significant meaning when it comes to developing a security plan. If cameras and extra lighting are installed in an attempt to thwart a hostile encounter, they will have little impact on an individual who does not intend to survive the day. Unlike the serious hazard of robbery, measures to monitor, record, or stop a violent invader will not work if an abuser who goes after the partner who left him intends to die. A small percentage of abusers in the study cited above made no effort to escape or even bargain with law enforcement immediately after the violent incident. Again, this points to a person who has no plans or intention of escaping. It demonstrates a single-minded desire to fulfill their single mission of revenge and ultimate control.

KNOWING WHEN AND WHERE

Two factors appear to be critical to developing a workplace security plan. As any security or protection professional would agree, knowing *when* and *where* an incident is likely to occur is indispensable to its prevention. A preliminary U.S. study of domestic assaults in the workplace since 2000 suggest that perhaps 56 percent of assaults occur as victims arrive at work or within one-half hour of the start of the shift. Approximately 9 percent happen at the end of the shift as the victim leaves or at some point during the work period. More studies are needed, but it does appear that the majority of known workplace assaults occur when the victim first arrives. We can infer that the abuser sets out to find the victim as soon as possible. If she or he is hiding in a shelter or some other unknown location, the first place the abuser knows the victim will be is at work, just where she or he has been for the past so-many years. This has clear implications for planning: If the police have only a small number of patrol cars and can provide a patrol for only one short period of time, perhaps the beginning of the shift is the most important time.

If there is reason to believe that the abuser is out to get the victim when she or he arrives at work, the most convenient place would be in the parking lot. This was clear in the Peace@Work study cited above; 30 percent of the attacks actually took place in the parking lot (and in some cases, other locations as well). The assault or verbal abuse in those situations started in the parking lot and ended when the victim fled inside and was killed or seriously assaulted. Why a parking lot? The perpetrator has few barriers and less chance of being interfered with in a parking lot. However, the incidents do not always start out violent. Parking lots are often where the victim and abuser begin an argument or discuss very private matters, where co-workers or clients cannot hear them. It is not uncommon for a worker without a private office to receive a personal visitor and take them outside to deal with the matter. Unfortunately, this discretion also increases their vulnerability: While the majority of incidents in the above study took place inside (46 percent), the range of industries and settings make the precise location of the violence difficult to classify. Office buildings, factory floors, and store counters all have been crime locations. The particular layout of each work facility needs to be considered when determining the best way to defend it.

The Peace@Work study does not encompass every assault or homicide. We clearly need more information. However, there appear to be trends. Additional studies should be done to reduce the growing numbers of victims and violent incidents in the workplace.

Target Hardening

If the decision has been made to protect the employee while she or he is working, a company has several options to lower the chances of an incident. Again, a threat assessment team will have to gauge risk and explore all options to determine what is feasible and what would be the most effective.

CHANGE THE VICTIM'S LOCATION OR SHIFT

There is at least one focus of the perpetrator's hostility, so make sure that the target victim is not where the abuser thinks she or he will be. They are or were once intimate partners, and it is not unusual for an abuser to know all the exact details of the victim's life. Find another location for the victim—one that the abuser is not able to get to easily, and the one with the least vulnerabilities. Try not to seclude or isolate the victim, but be sure you don't move the victim to the front lobby, immediately off the elevator, or near a window. If the victim works with the public, try to transfer her to another position, at least temporarily (in a back office, in an area not viewed by or accessible to the public, etc.). Depending on the size of the business, you might have to move her to a different office area, another floor, a different part of the plant, or even to another division of a company. There have been successful interventions within global corporations because victims could be transferred to another state to start whole new lives, free and safe from their abusers and still with the same job and benefits.

Smaller companies also have creative options. A victim can, for example, be switched to another shift. Perhaps the abuser can only harass and stalk their victim at certain times of the day or night. A simple change in shift can thwart his efforts to continue the abuse. Whatever the decision, it should reduce the opportunity for the abuser to reach the victim, but also be what is safest for the victim and co-workers. The key is to be innovative and creative in coming up with options; whether you are a small company or a large one, you can create a safer workplace for a threatened employee.

What you do obviously requires the support of the victim; work with her on any change in job, location, or shift. If management is truly empathetic and concerned, it will be easier to work together to determine new work duties, stations, and shifts. Your efforts have a greater chance of being successful when you have the agreement of the victim.

PARKING ARRANGEMENTS

Parking lots are places of vulnerability. There are few barriers, and they are rarely protected or guarded. A large number of murders and assaults occur right outside the facility, in the parking lot, when nobody is around.

General security improvements such as better lighting, additional security patrols, removal of concealing shrubbery, and even fencing will go a long way toward preventing all types of criminal activity. What can be done for the victim? Simple: Allow her to park in the safest spot (generally closest to the entrance). You or the general manager can give up designated parking space, the "Employee of the Month" parking space award can be postponed or donated, and even one of the handicapped parking spaces can be offered temporarily. If there is an underground garage with a security entrance, that might be the safest location.

But no matter where the victim is parked, she still has to leave her car to go inside (and then the reverse). Co-workers and supervisors go out of their way to escort the victim to and from her car. These are gallant gestures, but do the escorts have a plan should the abuser show up? Experts suggest that security guards provide the escort. If that is not possible, request a police patrol car for this dangerous time. (However, this might be possible only during a crisis.) If a co-worker or a supervisor escorts her to and from her car, it should only be done with a full understanding of the dangers and a pre-determined company plan of action should there be trouble.

Another good safety measure is to change the victim's vehicle. Using a rental or company car or swapping with a friend are all ways of eluding a stalker, who is probably going to be looking for the vehicle that he usually follows.

CELL PHONES

Giving the victim an activated cell phone might be the easiest and most valuable way to help. In fact, an emergency cell phone can be obtained from most human service or domestic violence agencies. Various telecommunications firms have made available cell phones that cannot receive calls but can make calls to a limited number of locations (i.e., the police, domestic violence agencies, or the courthouse). Having one can easily mean life or death for a victim of domestic violence who is confronted by her abuser in an isolated area—authorities can respond immediately. If you cannot obtain one from an agency, locally, an old cell phone will do. All cell phones are able to connect with 911, even if they are not currently in service with a wireless plan, as long as they are not broken and the location is within the range of the cell tower.

While we are on the topic of communication, it is a good idea to create a code word for a victim to use when they are in danger or need help. Imagine a situation where an abuser locates and corners his victim at work and delivers a litany of scolding and complaints. He doesn't allow her to leave, but she will certainly want to get help and will want somebody to know that something is wrong (without enraging the abuser). Perhaps she can tell him that she needs to cancel a meeting or needs to make a call for another reason. Having a code word to tell a co-worker, security guard, or supervisor can raise the alarm for help without raising the abuser's suspicion.

LOCK THE DOORS

Consider a lock-down during a critically dangerous period, or when the risk is great. It might look like a drastic step, but it is a good temporary option. Secure all doors and accessible windows and lock the entrances, especially any back doors the abuser might be aware of. Be sure you have easy egress in case of fire or other emergency. Such precautions will help protect the workplace in general from all types of threats or theft.

Consider also locking the front door and allowing entry only to valid visitors. This common procedure for high-risk and asset-vulnerable businesses such as jewelry stores is time-consuming, and you will have to assign a person to open the door and re-lock it, but it can work. (It might not be feasible for certain service industries that require convenient entry for customers and the public.) Posting a security guard at the main entrance might also seem like an extreme measure, but during a crisis period it will be helpful, particularly if the police are actively looking for an abuser-fugitive or there is reasonable cause to believe that he will come to the facility to commit violence.

GET OUT OF DODGE

Perhaps the safest thing to do is to simply remove the victim entirely. Do not fire her without thinking carefully about such a drastic step, because this can actually lead to a more dangerous workplace: Mistrust and secrecy among remaining employees will prevent them from reporting any new threats. Alternatively, an employer can give the victim time off to remove herself from all known locations—either by going to a domestic violence shelter, moving in with family or friends, or moving to an undisclosed location altogether. This last option is the safest for the victim if the threat has reached a lethal level. Consider a variety of scheduling options, such as vacation time, sick leave, or unpaid leave. As we explained in earlier chapters, having a job is extremely important if a victim of domestic abuse is to improve her or his circumstances, and the company benefits by keeping the worker on board. Your goal should be to make sure that the victim and the workplace are kept safe.

One particular domestic abuse situation involved an employee-victim who was considered to be a valued and important member of the company. The CEO decided to give this woman a company credit card and a phone card so that she could get away for a period of time. She left town, not entirely knowing where she was going. She stopped in a small coastal town, checked into a hotel, and called her boss to let him know that she was all right. She just stayed put for a few days, ordering room service and reflecting on her situation. Not only was it a chance for her to think and take a much-needed break, it was virtually impossible for the abuser to locate her and carry out his threat to kill her.

How long should the victim stay away? And when will the crisis be over? The truth is that there is no absolute way to determine when it will be safe again. Aside from the abuser being put in prison or dying, there is no way of knowing when to let the guard down. There are critical periods: right after a series of dire threats, the days just before or after a crucial court hearing, or after an aggravating turn of events that have made the abuser more volatile. Management needs to react immediately if it is to protect the workplace and its staff. Seek the advice of your security people, ask the victim what she or he thinks, and get a consensus of reasonable judgments before you decide when a victim should return to work.

Personal Safety Plans

If a company truly cares for its employees and wants to protect the significant financial investment it has made in orientation, training, and experience, it must show concern about the individual's safety when she is not at work. A crisis counselor can help a victim assess the threat and develop a personal safety plan. A large portion of such planning focuses on how to stay safe and make preparations to leave while she is still living with the abuser. Employers are strongly advised to make an agency referral and encourage the victim to work with such an authority; these professionals have the training and experience to handle this critical task. (See Appendix.)

Co-workers and supervisors must also be mindful of their own safety. The assessment should help identify other potential targets: Consider additional security when a threat has been made to someone who offered help to a victim, when the abuser has had an affair with a co-worker that might fuel his or her jealousy, or when, as in the Ferguson case, the company has already disciplined an employee for an act of domestic abuse or violence. All workers should take safety precautions at home and at work, and should seek the advice of the local police department.

Bringing in Outside Help

Get expert help if you believe the company does not have the capability, resources, or expertise to deal with the threat. (The overall risk assessment, conducted before there was any threat, should have determined this.) It is always advisable to contact and collaborate with local police, but individual officers are not usually security experts, and they have other community responsibilities. An outside consultant can develop a comprehensive and detailed assessment, and can also do the security planning. Some consultants use private investigators to gather information about the threat and monitor the abuser's activities to verify that he or she is indeed a danger and even to try to discover what is being planned. If an abuser spends his entire time staking out the work site, running to the liquor store, and practicing at the firing range, the company will certainly want and need to know.

Ask trusted colleagues to make referrals. Ask to see the security firm's references and industry credentials, and be sure to verify that the information is accurate. Good security firms are expensive. Management must determine what its budget will handle, based on how committed it is to ensuring the safety of its people. Previous chapters have pointed out the liability risks related to negligence when it comes to protecting the workforce. Keep them in mind.

Another source of outside help: a private security agency that can assign a guard to monitor the facility. If the company does not already have its own internal security department, hiring a uniformed guard at the facility will make employees feel a lot safer (and might discourage an abuser from entering the property). Use the same process you used to hire a consultant to find the best security guards. For a truly dangerous situation, I advise you to have armed guards who are able to respond to any firepower threat. In many locations, you also have the option of hiring an off-duty police officer to act as security. The advantages to this are that the officer is in uniform, commanding a higher level of respect and authority. Off-duty officers maintain communication with other police departments, so there will be a quick response when a call goes in for back-up support. An off-duty police officer working private security can still make an arrest, carry a firearm, and in some cases park their patrol car right in front of the business.

Be aware that police or guard presence can frighten employees and create anxiety. Just remember that if the threat is credible, it is far more important to have a decisive and authoritative resource on hand to counter such a hazard than to keep up appearances. There have probably been rumors about the threat anyway; seeing a security guard will relieve some of your employees' private fears, despite whatever is said openly.

How long should you keep a guard there? Cost, impact on safety, and the value of feeling more secure are just some of the factors that need to be weighed. Again, when you have reason to believe that there is an imminent threat, take these stronger security measures.

A Response Plan

First, be on the lookout for the abuser. Who do you want to be responsible for this crucial task? The security guard or other individuals responsible for providing protection must be told to keep an eye out for the perpetrator. Security personnel should have the training and experience to know how to stay observant and aware of suspicious activity. Unfortunately some employers forget this; their "lookout" is a receptionist who has other duties besides monitoring the entrance or the parking lot. In many organizations, the receptionist must answer phones, direct visitors and clients, and provide other administrative assistance. Assign someone else to do *only* this lookout task, and have a back-up should the first person be out.

Should you warn everyone? If you notify every employee about a potentially threatening person, you can be accused of slander or libel (especially if flyers and warnings are freely passed around, identifying the abuser as a deranged killer). There has to be a reasonable justification for providing people with these details, but it might be enough just to remind employees in general to notify security if any non-workers are in prohibited areas and to keep visitors out of restricted areas. Check this out with the company's legal counsel.

The individual who is assigned this notification task (and their back-up) must have what people need in order to identify the abuser, including a description and photograph of the abuser as well as his motor vehicle. It is far better to be able to identify the abuser as he or she pulls into the parking lot than after he has entered the building. A discreetly-placed flyer, with descriptions and pictures, can list action steps and numbers to call. (The options will vary, depending on the facility and exact situation.) While the threat management team is developing a plan to secure the facility, notify law enforcement, and communicate with employees, be sure they cover all the important areas, such as those outlined in the next section.

SECURE THE FACILITY

If the staff is fortunate enough to have advance warning that the abuser is on his way and might be violent or has been spotted near the facility, consider locking all entrances. This general security measure can immediately prevent the abuser from entering. Someone who is armed can easily blow open a door or blast apart a glass door, but locking entrances can buy you time and even discourage access.

NOTIFY POLICE

If there is an active restraining or trespass order, the abuser's approach is enough for police to respond. Those employees in charge of contacting the police should have a copy of the order. Obviously, the presence of any weapon or threatening behavior should be reported to the emergency operator; this, too, should get the police to respond. If there are no protective orders or legal mandates and there is no clear sign of threat, police might not respond (it would be no different than someone walking into a store). Police commit their resources to actual crimes occurring or that have occurred; this is why you must develop a relationship with the local police department. If an officer is familiar with the case and the facility and knows that the person coming to the facility is a real threat, he or she is more likely to respond quickly.

NOTIFY ALL EMPLOYEES

You don't want to cause people to panic, but you should let employees know that there is a danger. How you do this will depend on the layout of the facility and the communication equipment available. You can use the PA system, e-mail, or speakerphones to get the word out (if there is imminent danger, don't use e-mail). Crisis preparation for any type of emergency (industrial accidents, violence, terrorism, etc.) will require quick and effective notification to employees. One note of caution: Some people suggest pulling the fire alarm if there is a shooting. Purposely detailing this step in a response plan is risky, because it might put more people into the line of fire by sending them outside the building, as opposed to warning them of the true danger.

If the perpetrator is prowling around outside, employees should be warned to stay away from windows and doors. If he is already inside, the situation is much more tenuous. One option is to escape through a pre-determined exit. Another option is to instruct people to lock themselves in individual offices and put up barricades.

Obviously, it is critical to notify the victim that the abuser is arriving, since he is probably after her. Be sure she is told what to do and where to go or hide.

ACTUAL VIOLENCE

It is extremely hard to know precisely how to respond or what to do should someone open fire, because so much is unpredictable. There will be general confusion and volatility. The one valuable suggestion is also the most ironic: Stay calm! Panic limits reasoning, leading to poor choices and further problems.

Do anticipate trauma and chaos. The focus of this book is on preventing and managing domestic violence in the workplace, but take advantage of current and comprehensive resources to help you plan your critical-incident response. **Preparation for a critical incident must cover staff responsibility and accountability, access to emergency services, communication with employees and their families, trauma response, media relations, and contingencies operations.**

Working with the Victim

It is vital that you work with the victim. In many instances, victims are true survival experts who have held on to their very lives by learning how to judge the reactions of their abuser. The employee-victim does not have to be at every threat management team meeting nor be part of every decision, but this person can provide vital information: how the perpetrator is likely to respond if, say, criminal charges are filed; what the abuser is likely to be doing at a particular time; and his level of stability. If the rest of the abuser's life seems to be deteriorating, consider the likelihood that he might be willing to throw it all away in a violent explosion.

Some of the measures you need to take will affect the victim's life and job, such as a transfer to another shift, time off, or a change in duties. Your essential focus has to be on the safety of all your employees, but by all means, consider the victim's needs. If they are not addressed or the victim believes she is not being treated fairly, she might not provide the information you need. Other abuse victims will be watching to see how you handle the situation, and might decide not to report or disclose their own concerns. This might put the company at greater risk.

Documenting Security Measures and Incidents

Documentation is extremely critical. Keep a written record of every threat made to the lives of your employees, and document every assessment, decision, and measure you take related to the threat.

Documenting threats and the company's own actions provides a record you can review to determine the workplace vulnerabilities. Recording such information can help identify trends and show the importance of putting resources and time into workplace safety. You and your security and human resources personnel will be amazed at the number of reports and disclosures that you will hear about after you implement a domestic violence safety program. Certainly, the development of a program does not itself instigate the increase of occurrences; it simply reveals how common the issue is. Remember that it is better to have the incidents and concerns disclosed and addressed than to let a stewing crisis explode unexpectedly. The documentation can also be used to assess the strength and weaknesses of your threat management program.

It's also very important to have documentation in case there is a court hearing. It can be used as evidence; a written record of incidents, for example, can support the prosecution of a stalking case. However, such record-keeping can also protect the company from a civil suit should there be violence. If a company can demonstrate how the threat was promptly assessed and what efforts were made to protect employees, it is less likely to pay negligence claims. However, the crucial point is not to protect the company from a lawsuit, but to prevent an incident. Use your legal counsel to decide what you should document. Once again, a note of caution: If a threat has been investigated and you decide not to take extensive measures, this might be all the prosecution needs to show failure to protect. Any decision you make not to take certain security measures must be detailed in the records and substantiated with valid reasons.

Conclusion

Your responsibility is to make the workplace and your staff as safe as possible. To do that, you must assess how vulnerable you are to workplace violence and assess the company's ability to successfully manage risks in terms of facility protections and procedures. Develop a relationship with the local police department, which can provide advice as well as personnel during a violent incident. Secure the grounds and the facilities through environmental design and technology. Seek legal protection through civil and criminal court systems. Protect the victim, and gather information about the abuser. Gather and provide evidence for any court trials. Create a threat assessment team to determine whether or not there is an extreme and likely chance of violence (and by whom), and bring an additional layer of security. Finally, develop a response plan and make sure everyone knows how it works. Outline what needs to be done by whom and when, should the perpetrator come to the workplace. Consider such things as the cost of specific action, what resources are available, any impact that security measures will have on company operations (and their actual effectiveness). Document everything, and by all means, err on the side of caution when it comes to staff and victim protection.

Chapter 9
Policy Development

An organization's position on any given issue is based on company policy. This is where employees learn what is expected of them and what they can expect from the company. Company policy needs to be flexible enough to apply to a variety of situations, yet clearly outline what is prohibited and how management will support and protect its employees. The language used in a domestic violence policy must be carefully constructed so that it is comprehensible to every employee, yet easily defensible should the policy be brought into court as evidence. The recommendations in this chapter and the resources included in the Appendix will help you select the policy that best meets the needs of your organization.

This chapter will cover key policy considerations, such as:

▲ Who should be part of the policy development team?
▲ How can the policy encourage collaboration between employees and management?
▲ Should there be a separate domestic policy regarding violence?
▲ How can a domestic violence component be integrated into a general workplace violence policy?
▲ How should the policy be disseminated?
▲ What are the specific components of an effective policy?
▲ How can we adopt and alter a model policy to fit our needs?

A model policy appears in the Appendix.

Who should be involved?

You will need to assemble a diverse group of individuals to fully assess a risk and determine appropriate safety measures. Policy development should also be done by a diverse group of individuals. Representatives from human resources, security, upper management, and the health and safety departments can unite to provide all the unique perspectives needed in such a process. This chapter will provide model language and suggestions, but it must not replace the careful and committed consideration you will get from key people in the development of this important document.

Consider inviting a representative from the local domestic violence agency even if it is for just one meeting. She or he can make specific recommendations as to what community resources are available, and can provide valuable expertise regarding the dynamics and issues surrounding domestic violence.

Legal Considerations

Legal counsel is a vital component of any policy-development team, as the resulting document will be closely scrutinized if there is a court case. Careful consideration may prevent or reduce any potential liability suits. Attorneys have a different perspective than security or employee-relations personnel. There may be disagreements regarding what or who is to be protected (the employee-victims, the workplace in general, the financial stability of the company, etc.). A company attorney will likely advise against using language that too specifically describes any obligation of the company, in order to reduce your liability. Having any policy at all on domestic violence in the workplace can create a vulnerability for an employer should an employee become injured or suffer some disciplinary action; an attorney can write a disclaimer stating that the supportive and protective measures are only guidelines for management and do not constitute any guarantee or contract between the company and its employees. A disclaimer, however, should not weaken or nullify a genuine effort to address the issue; the best defense against any charge that you have failed to follow policy is to actually carry out and fulfill any stated actions or procedures. Therefore, any statements as to how often training will occur or how incidents will be reported and documented must be carefully considered and must be realistically attainable.

If there is any question about whether it is more important to protect the assets of the company or to provide support to employees, the deciding factor should always be the physical safety of all personnel. In fact, this is the essential goal of the policy and the corresponding program.

Employee Endorsement and Support

Many human resource professionals are proficient and familiar with policy development, but you need the support and "buy-in" of everyone if you are to make it truly effective. This initiative genuinely needs to be one of collaboration between the employees and management. A policy is not a simple list of rules enforced by the company through threat of punishment. While it is important to clearly define what will not be tolerated and what can have disciplinary consequences, the company must demonstrate its commitment to protect and support its employees.

Safety cannot and should not be guaranteed. Employers can always offer assistance to all victims of violent crime, including domestic violence victims. The policy should positively and proactively empower all staff to prevent any possible violence by encouraging people to report any concerns to a supervisor or management. Knowing that a victim will be supported makes participation all the more likely.

Stand-Alone Policy, or a Component of a Broader Policy?

An important consideration to be made in adopting and developing a domestic violence policy is to determine if it will be a stand-alone policy or a component of a general policy on workplace violence. There are merits to both approaches: A separate, stand-alone policy sends a clear message about how seriously the company takes the issue. A separate chapter in the policy manual draws more attention to the company's commitment to support victims and denounce acts of abuse. Be sure to also have a general policy on workplace violence to accompany and complement any measures or protocol laid out in the domestic violence policy. There needs to be a system for reporting, assessing, and responding to threats and acts of violence. **All organizations of any reasonable size should have a workplace policy to help prevent violence of any kind**, and many companies have taken further steps to address workplace violence. (The subject of violence is covered at length in many other books, so it will not be covered here. It is the subject of *domestic violence* that progressive businesses are now taking measures to address.)

If there is a workplace violence policy already in place, it is easy to insert language and principles for a domestic violence component. By adding a domestic violence section to an established workplace violence policy, you imply that it is a legitimate and dangerous threat, which might help streamline the response to any identified threat. It also allows you to easily combine dissemination and training components with general efforts to prevent workplace violence. Throughout the document, components can be added that augment and make the general workplace violence policy more comprehensive. Essentially, by broadening the definition of what constitutes *workplace violence*, the coverage is much more thorough, and therefore more effective.

To incorporate a domestic violence policy into an existing policy on workplace violence, make clear in the initial policy statement that the goal is to protect employees from all sources of threat—not just from co-workers, but from people outside of the organization. Abusive intimate partners (former and present) can be specifically identified as sources of danger, along with strangers and hostile clients or customers. A section-by-section approach can illustrate where these components can be inserted. We will say more about this later in the chapter.

The term *domestic violence* should be defined in the definitions section of the policy. The verbiage provided in the model policy can be inserted into an existing or newly developed workplace violence document. Under "prohibited actions," again make it clear that threatening, harassing, or violent behavior toward anyone, not just co-workers, will not be tolerated. There may be certain circumstances where even off-duty conduct will affect an individual's position in the company.

The most crucial part of the policy that applies to victims of abuse will be the section on support and protection. If there is violence in the workplace from a robbery or a co-worker assault, an employee might need to take work time for medical appointments or court dates. The domestic violence victim's situation is different because the violent incident often takes place away from the workplace. However, the impact of this violence will probably affect the employee's attendance and performance more than other types of crime, largely due to the fact that their entire life is in upheaval.

Components of the Policy

The model policy offered in the Appendix has several components, each with its own characteristics and purpose. Let's look at the key points for each of the sections. A policy should include:

- ▲ A purpose or mission statement
- ▲ A list of definitions
- ▲ A description of prohibited actions
- ▲ A description of actions that management will take
- ▲ A non-retaliation and confidentiality clause
- ▲ A list of responsibilities (by position or department)

THE PURPOSE

An initial statement should depict the reason and purpose of the policy. If there is any misunderstanding as to why businesses should adopt measures to address domestic violence in the workplace, be sure you describe the financial impact and physical risk of domestic violence on an individual business. This section outlines the official position of the company: it demonstrates support for victims and holds abusers accountable for their actions. It is the strongest way a company can convey an unmistakable message to employees, clients, and the public at large. This is also where you can add a disclaimer regarding guarantees or suggestions that every case will be handled similarly or specifically.

DEFINITIONS

The definitions section serves to make certain that all parties fully understand what is considered to be domestic violence, and spells out where and to whom the policies apply. Behaviors can be specifically described in order to convey clear expectations of what employees should or should not do, but only after careful consideration is given to the language used to describe actions and persons involved. If the policy is ever scrutinized in court, ambiguous or misleading terms will likely be a problem. Domestic violence is more than just physical violence, as we have said throughout this book; the complete pattern of abuse needs to be described when identifying these cases, including sexual, financial, social, and emotional damage.

Should you refer to same-sex domestic relationships in a company policy? You should avoid any suggestion that you are endorsing or condemning these kinds of relationships, but it is crucial that you address these relationships just as seriously as conventional relationships, especially when there is a threat to the workplace. It does not matter what the personal opinion of the employer is on the subject; a partner in a homosexual relationship can threaten the workplace if she or he is an abuser. In fact, there might be a greater need for you to show support for the victim, since she or he might have to come out of the closet when disclosing their abusive situation.

PROHIBITED ACTIONS

A section listing prohibited actions spells out what will be considered acceptable conduct, and provides the grounds for any disciplinary action that can result from a violation of these guidelines. Although there are laws making such violent behavior illegal, a company that makes a pronouncement that such abuse is wrong reinforces the message. This ripples through the community, thereby increasing awareness and strengthening the movement to denounce family violence.

What about acts of abuse that are committed off company property and/or during non-work hours? In general, a company has little leeway over the behavior of its employees when they are not at work. The nature of the criminal act, the employee's unique responsibilities, and the potential impact the behavior has on the company are exceptions to the rule. Organizations that employ mental health professionals or security officers should consider notifying their employees of their obligation to behave accordingly at all times on or off duty. (See Chapter 4 on batterers in the workplace.)

SUPPORT

Consider having a section outlining which services and support there are for victims of abuse. This will show that the organization cares about its employees. Areas to be addressed include allowances for time off, changes to benefits, and security measures that can be developed to help prevent any harassment or violence from occurring in the workplace.

This section should also list Employee Assistance Program contact information (if available) as well as the name, address, and phone numbers for all local domestic violence service providers and the phone number for the national referral line.

But what commitments are implied in this expression of support? Do not get too specific, because they can't all be guaranteed for every case. Insert a general statement and a list of suggested supports to address a particular situation. Essentially, management will always want to have the discretion, within legal parameters, to decide what course of action it will take. This is not to detract from the supportive spirit of the policy: Supervisors and HR people must be committed to addressing the problem and must make valid efforts to help and understand the trials that victims and what they are facing. Otherwise, the policy will be regarded as a piece of paper with no substance, and the employer will eventually lose credibility. Consider each case separately, and take the best course of action. Keep in mind how the decision will affect general employee morale. In deciding what to do, remember to provide the same benefits and services to all employees—there should be no discrepancies as to what is offered from one employee to the next. You do not want to be charged with discrimination.

ANTI-RETALIATION AND CONFIDENTIALITY

It is vital that you encourage employees to report concerns. One way to get employees to feel more comfortable about reporting concerns is to place a non-retaliation and confidentiality clause in the policy. This clause will reassure employees that an honest attempt to report a concern or disclose their abusive relationship will not backfire and result in any negative repercussions.

Employees will also feel more inclined to report an incident or threat if they know that their identity will be protected. However, it is important to realize that absolute confidentiality cannot always be guaranteed. Management must make every effort to protect anonymity and disclosure information, but safety considerations always override any obligation to maintain privacy. The rule of thumb is to disclose information solely on a need-to-know basis; consider asking your company's attorney to elaborate on this subject or approve certain disclosures beforehand.

Reports of abuse can be misleading or simply not true. If an employee is falsely identified as a victim or an abuser because of another person's malicious objectives or misguided suspicions, first determine that there is no valid case of domestic violence. Then decide, whether the person doing the reporting had mistaken intentions or was deliberately deceiving you. In the case of the latter, disciplinary action would be appropriate (as it would be for any dishonest behavior in the workplace).

RESPONSIBILITIES

Finally, to further expand on the specific responsibilities of various staff members and departments, spell out what is expected of all parties. Not only does this serve to give clear steps and protocol for individual members of the organization, but it also shows how everyone is responsible for maintaining the safety of the entire workforce—not just the security and risk-management people.

Dissemination

Finally, a policy is only effective when all employees are aware of it and understand the scope and meaning of the message. Once company leadership signs off on the policy, there should be some internal announcement of its incorporation into the personnel manual. A range of training programs should be scheduled immediately for all staff. New employees should be oriented to this policy, as with all other company rules and protocol. Some companies have their employees sign a document stating that they have read and understand the policy. This promotes a level of commitment, and reduces the possibility that someone will claim that they were not aware of the existence or meaning of the policy. Signing your name to a piece of paper adds to the level of obligation to the act, and sends a clear message of support to possible victims. It also forces batterers to realize that their behavior is not acceptable and won't be tolerated. It is crucial that you follow all outlined steps describing how employees will be informed of this policy faithfully; any failure to do so can create a legal liability if it is brought up in court.

Adopting a Policy

A model policy can be found in the Appendix. A policy is purposely simple and short. Broad, comprehensive policies are often easier to manage and interpret. (If you are too specific, there will be no end to the list of appropriate behaviors or responsibilities.) Individual businesses vary considerably, but the model we provide here can be adapted. Policy development team members should be free to modify, expand, and edit this document to fit the particular needs and culture of the company.

Smaller companies that do not have individual departments such as Human Resources or security might assign management personnel to these roles and responsibilities. If this is the case, community agencies and national organizations can be invaluable allies. Excellent resources for model policies can be found in the Appendix sections at the end of this book.

Conclusion

There are a great many sample policies available from local shelters and from the national organizations listed in the Appendix. Careful consideration should be given to the development of any policy and in implementation and actual compliance. To paraphrase a statement from Kim Wells, executive director of the Corporate Alliance to End Partner Violence, the best thing to do is to develop a good policy, and then follow through with what is outlined. Having a policy but failing to implement it consistently defeats its purpose and exposes the company to lawsuits that can conceivably send it into bankruptcy. But no matter how much consideration goes into writing a policy covering domestic violence, it is vital that you immediately train all employees at every level to make certain that everyone understands its purpose and their own obligations and responsibilities.

Chapter 10
Training

I was picking up my presentation materials and disconnecting the laptop after another supervisor workshop on domestic violence in the workplace when I noticed someone standing off to the side. It was a participant who had listened very intently to all that I said but did not ask questions or make any comments. I had a feeling during the session that she wanted to say something but was waiting. After most of the other participants had left the room, she came up to me. It seemed that she was struggling for a way to start the conversation, so I just asked her if she thought that the workshop was of any value.

"Oh, yes," she said. *"I think it opened a lot of people's eyes."* The woman went on to tell me how she really hoped that her colleagues took what I said to heart and how important the subject was. I asked her if she had ever worked with someone whose personal situation concerned her, and she shook her head no. After a brief moment of silence, she shared what she was holding back. *"That was me. I was one of those people who did not know how to tell my boss what was happening. I was so scared but could not afford to lose my job. He was doing all that he could to cause me to quit or to get them to fire me until I could not take it any more. I finally left—I even left the state. I really liked that job, and I wanted to stay. It was so hard starting over."*

She described her struggle to find a new place to live and start all over again at a new agency. She told me how she found support through a non-profit agency from domestic-violence victim advocates, but she never thought she would be able to talk to her employer, former or current. She said, *"You don't know how often I thought about telling my boss about why I was coming in late or why I was getting so upset after my husband called. I just couldn't. I just didn't think they would understand."*

She then thanked me for presenting the workshop and explaining to her colleagues why it is so important to be aware of what a victim might be going through. I just shook her hand and told her that it was nothing compared to what *she* had accomplished. And it really isn't.

The Importance of Training

We've talked so far about the rise in domestic violence and the struggle of victims to hold on to their jobs, their dignity, and their lives as they deal with what is happening. Now we turn to the role of staff training and awareness. No matter how well-developed the policies and response plans, they will just be filed away and forgotten unless all employees understand the problem and what the company intends to do to prevent violence in the workplace. Without training, victims will still be reluctant to come forward and the risks of a violent incident will continue to increase.

In many ways, training is the only real cost of a program package. Aside from the time it takes to adapt model policies and plans such as the ones outlined in the book or referred to in the Appendix, the most costly expenditure is likely to be training the staff. You can contract a professional trainer, but a training program can be developed internally, with the assistance of the local advocacy agency. Either way, it might take some creative scheduling so that employees can attend the training, but training your employees (especially supervisors) is a crucial component in the development of any program. Online programs and educational materials can be effective and valuable, but the face-to-face interaction with a good trainer will engage participants and challenge them to think.

Once the domestic abuse training is underway, it will be clear to all that it won't be like explaining the company's new dental plan. The subject is a very sensitive and emotionally arousing one that will probably elicit a wide range of responses. Many business leaders and some staff members will not understand why domestic abuse is a workplace issue; some will state outright that it is a personal matter best left to counselors and the courts. Those who are more intimately familiar with domestic abuse will have even stronger responses. Some people will not want to go at all.

In this chapter, we will explain why and how you must train your employees on domestic violence protocol. We will describe different types of training for different levels of responsibility and emphasize ways to collaborate with outside agencies that will prove to be vital resources as individual sensitivity surrounding these issues emerges during the program. Managing adverse reactions, using humor in training, and choosing the audiovisual material that will be useful in a formal program will all be discussed.

Who should undergo training?

All employees, no matter what the position or salary grade, should go through the training because every level of an organization will be affected by a domestic violence situation. Once policies have been developed and response plans have been approved, announcements should go out to all employees via memos, the intranet, or hard-copy addendum to the personnel manual. Frontline employees must know the purpose of the policy, the sanctions outlined, what the company will provide in the way of support and protection, and how employees can disclose or make a report.

All new employees must be told about the program and the policies during orientation. This has the added value of letting employees know from the very beginning what behavior will not be tolerated and how the company can be of help. Do not underestimate the importance of setting a tone right at the beginning that yours is an environment of mutual dignity and respect for all employees. Have each employee (old and new) sign a statement that they have read and understand the policy, and keep this in their personnel file.

EMPLOYEES

In most businesses, the people who are most aware of what is going on are the frontline employees—those who operate the machinery, interact with the clients, or actually produce the product or provide the service that is the basis for the business. These are the people who will probably be in direct contact with the victim (and perhaps the abuser). A separate training program on domestic abuse is ideal, but the subject can be added to the general training about workplace violence, safety, or another health-related topic. If managers or supervisors balk when their staff are pulled from the production floor or the office cubicles, remind them that these are the people who will be the first to know about a problem.

TRAINING

The employer is a very influential force in every worker's life. Taking a stance on the issue reinforces the idea that such abusive behavior is socially not acceptable. Training broadens and underlines the community's efforts to increase awareness of family violence and condemn this criminal activity.

Make all employees aware of the company's stance on abusers. Whether you cover it in general workplace violence training or in any program specifically designated for domestic violence, this will be a very hard topic to introduce, because male participants often feel insulted and personally attacked. Emphasize the actual behaviors that are prohibited while at work, rather than delve into people's private lives. Men with sensitive positions need to be aware of their additional responsibility, even when they are not at work. Carefully handle all discussions surrounding gender roles in abuse.

What should such employee training cover?

1. **What is in the policy.** In many ways, your policy is not about what employees should or should not do, but it does emphasize that the company is aware of what might affect their lives. Explain how the policy will help them; this might be the most beneficial, memorable message that a company can communicate. It will instill loyalty and a sense of community.
2. **The warning signs, dynamics of abuse, and resources available to domestic violence victims.** This kind of information should be understood so that employees can provide support and encouragement.
3. **The proper means of reporting any threats of violence.** The process of reporting and documenting should be covered, but there needs to be discussion during training about why employees resist telling a supervisor (embarrassment, fear of retaliation, not wanting to get involved).
4. **The company's no-tolerance policy.** Clearly explain to employees that any abusive or criminal behavior at work will not be tolerated, whether it is against co-workers, clients, family, or acquaintances.
5. **The role of the employee-threat assessment.** All staff members, especially frontline employees such as receptionists and security personnel, must be made aware of their responsibilities in developing and implementing safety measures.

SUPERVISORS

Supervisors are in the forefront when it comes to managing and monitoring the production and performance of employees. It is crucial to make their training relevant and engaging, and to prepare to manage the domestic-abuse issues that will confront them in the workplace. Managers or human resource people will probably become involved only after the supervisor learns of any problems with an employee's performance or of any concerns that there might be violence. Supervisor training must cover the impact of an incident on the company, its relevance to workplace production, and safety measures. A thorough review of the company policy must also be conducted.

The key focus of supervisor training is to make supervisors aware of the warning signs of an employee-victim or an employee-batterer. Job performance issues such as tardiness or frequent mistakes will naturally lead a supervisor to consider evaluating the individual's job performance or even taking disciplinary action. It is during such times that supervisors usually decide that abuse is the root cause of the deteriorating performance because there are likely to be unmistakable indications of physical assault (black eyes, bruises, etc.).

The point I want to stress is that the obvious and stereotypical signs of abuse might not be readily apparent, but astute supervisors will notice other indications. Trainers should provide examples of how the abusive relationship affects a victim's emotions and behavior; this will broaden the supervisor's understanding of what domestic abuse consists of.

Making people aware of the problem and the various warning signs is the first part of supervisor training. This is followed by discussions on how to approach the employee-victim or employee-batterer. Many supervisors will be reluctant to talk to an employee about such a personal matter; trainers can make two good points to relieve them of these reservations. First, it is the supervisor's responsibility to talk to an employee about job performance. If it is a genuine attempt to solve the problem and assist the employee, the employee might talk about the crisis. Second, trainers must emphasize that by no means are supervisors obligated to act as counselors or advocates: All they have to do is make a referral. There is no need to get into the details of the abuse or act as confidant.

The last part of supervisor training is to review how the supervisor can help the victim or the batterer. Supervisors have the most influence when it comes to the employee's ability to take time off. All the alternatives and options should be covered. It might be necessary to explain to supervisors why it is so important to provide the employee-victim or the employee-batterer with the time off to get counseling or tend to their personal matters, and why it is so important for the policy to outline the important reasons for supporting victims. Human resources staff often deal with some of these measures, but supervisors should still be knowledgeable enough to make suggestions to their employees and follow through.

Let me stress one very important point: If there is any concern or threat of actual violence occurring in the workplace supervisors must understand how important it is to pass along any knowledge of a possible threat to the HR department and managers as soon as possible. A veteran supervisor who has done an excellent job maintaining a productive workforce while handling a variety of crises might feel confident of their ability to assess the risk of violence and deal with it themselves. This is an extremely dangerous attitude: the supervisor *must* pass along every warning sign of impending violence to the crisis management team or upper management. A good supervisor should be able to connect one warning sign to other warning signs indicated at another branch or location of the company, but in too many situations, managers are notified only after things get volatile and it is too late to take preventative measures. **No matter how skilled and trusted a supervisor thinks he or she is, any possibility of workplace violence erupting *has* to be passed on to every department and individual who needs to know.** The procedure should be discussed in detail during training.

There should not be any official negative consequences for making a report. Supervisors and managers must feel that they can make a report without feeling that they should deal with the problem themselves. It must be made clear that failing to pass along such information to management jeopardizes the company's safety, but you must also tell them that failing to report can affect their standing and promotional potential.

As for the supervisor's role in an actual threat that violence might erupt at work, this should be reviewed during training. An overview of threat assessment and how to determine which security measures should be taken can be included, with special emphasis placed on their role and responsibilities.

Training the Crisis Management Team

Perhaps the most in-depth and comprehensive training will be reserved for those who will be responsible for assessing their risk and determining security measures in the event of an actual workplace threat. The crisis management team is the company's high-level body charged with investigating cases. This team of experienced professionals from diverse backgrounds can draw on their comprehensive knowledge and skills to consider all the legal, physical, human, and economic aspects of a workplace threat, but few of these experts will have specific knowledge of violence prevention and management.

Their training must go beyond simple lectures to encompass more-engaging, case study exercises and discussions with domestic-violence advocates. As for the specific skills of investigation, interviews, assessments, and other competencies, consider using a professional consultant for this program. Quite simply, HR staff members can develop and deliver the basic message to supervisors and staff, but highly sensitive and intensive threat-management training should be conducted by those most qualified. Domestic violence is a pervasive threat; the typical one-hour gloss-over will hardly be sufficient.

The components of training for crisis management include the basic elements provided to supervisors and frontline employees, as well as the team's unique responsibilities. Areas that should be covered:

1. **Impact and risk.** A thorough analysis of domestic violence workplace incidents should be done to identify trends, risk factors, and probable indicators. Special attention can be given to liability issues such as negligence in not responding to a threat, repercussions of any disciplinary actions, and precautions regarding grounds for charges of defamation or slander.

2. **Team protocol.** The exact working procedures of the team need to be identified: Who will lead the process? How will you contact each other in an emergency? What

circumstances call for a meeting? What and how should you document?

3. **Threat assessment.** The protocol regarding how to investigate should be presented: the kinds of background checks; who to interview and how to conduct the interviews; indicators of imminent violence; and various predictors of violence.

4. **Resources.** The team must identify and know how to work with company and community resources, including domestic violence service providers, the Employee Assistance Program (if available), law enforcement personnel, mental health professionals, and even security consultants.

5. **Action steps.** Even before an investigation is over, the company might need to take protective measures. The range and feasibility of disciplinary actions (for batterers) and security measures can be explored in training.

6. **Crisis response.** This team must be prepared to control the crisis if there is an incident. Emergency management, employee and asset accountability, family notification, communication with employees and the media, critical incident debriefing, and business continuity are all elements that the team needs to be familiar with.

7. **Case studies.** The team should be able to "practice" before there is a real crisis. Fictitious situations or actual incidents gleaned from media reports can provide the case studies for the team to practice how they respond. An excellent way to do this is to provide a longitudinal format so that the team sequentially responds to specific events (in a continuum) of an unfolding case. This method is better than just practicing steps, because the team members can learn how each person reacts and considers case details. Any disagreements or contradictory views must be identified in practice, before a real incident occurs.

One training session is not enough, and having just an initial meeting to consecrate the policy is inadequate. Hold regular crisis management meetings (preferably quarterly) and conduct additional training using current information so that the subject remains relevant and the team players are familiar with their perspective roles. A review of previous cases and relevant incidents from other companies can keep a crisis management team alert and prepared for potential threats. Crisis management is now a priority for businesses in many areas; regional associations of professionals responsible for crisis management are being formed across the country so that people can network, share resources, and develop skills.

Training Resources

HR professionals do not usually have the time to adequately research and develop training programs. Products and other resources on the subject of domestic violence in the workplace are limited, although this is changing. The same consultant who is training the crisis management team might also be able to offer training to other staff members, but consider the individual's direct experience in domestic violence training and familiarity with the issue before you contract someone. As we have emphasized throughout this book, the threat from domestic violence is quite different from other forms of workplace violence. It is important to get someone who has the expertise.

Video is a popular training medium. I strongly suggest that you only use videos to *supplement* your instruction, however. A quality training video can indeed provide engaging case studies and it is often the most popular part of the training program, but it should not be all there is.

Online learning is especially effective in larger companies or organizations where there is limited time or space for a physical gathering of employees. The merits of such delivery formats and the ease of tracking are attractive, but online training has its limitations. Domestic violence is such a deeply personal and complicated issue; interaction and immediate Q and A sessions, so important for this emotionally charged training, are not possible through a computer screen. Online learning is still a useful option; just as with videos, it is an excellent way to supplement a live, participatory training program or review what has been learned.

Partnering for Training Delivery

WORKING WITH LAW ENFORCEMENT AGENCIES

Most police departments have officers who routinely speak to the communities they serve about crime prevention. These agencies know the lethality and complexity of domestic violence cases, and can thus provide a crucial component of a training program. Many agencies have officers especially knowledgeable about what victims of abuse endure and what resources are available to them. Perhaps what is most valuable is just their simple presence: If a police officer describes the range of criminal laws that have to do with domestic abuse cases wearing badge and uniform, he or she makes a clear and undeniable statement that domestic violence is a crime—not a simple lover's quarrel. A domestic violence call is a serious concern to responding officers, and they will be able to describe how dangerous such cases are better than almost anyone else.

WORKING WITH SHELTERS

If the subject of domestic violence appears daunting or complicated to staff-development personnel, the good news is that there are community educators ready to help. Another option to consider is to have the professional-development staff go through the volunteer training provided by battered women's shelters. This will provide the most in-depth learning, and the benefits of collaboration are many. Despite misperceptions and stereotypes that these agencies are full of man-hating radicals trying to break up families, the reality is that these agencies are professionally run. Key personnel (who generally have graduate degrees) direct their programs to optimal performance. There are even certification programs validating the professionalism of these advocates. These programs are often well established with strong positions in political and community networks, especially in metropolitan areas, and they are solid players.

A company benefits in many ways when it works with such entities. Firstly, it is an opportunity for management and the agency to work together and develop a relationship. This partnership will prove invaluable if there is an actual incident. In terms of the training, the agency advocate can handle areas where they have the most expertise, as well as conduct the segments on the dynamics of domestic violence and the services they provide. This is a very sensitive subject; since agency people work directly with victims, they can best elaborate on the important aspects and make the subject more understandable. The question of why a victim stays with her abuser is best explained by professionals who deal with this issue on a daily basis.

Secondly, the agency will be able to explain exactly what programs and services they can offer to a victim, as well as what is available throughout the community and beyond. The court system, victim units within the local law enforcement agency, housing programs, legal aid, and credit counseling are all programs and services that they will have a working familiarity with.

Involving a domestic violence agency in the training program provides a third purpose: it is a direct way to reach victims of abuse who happen to be sitting in the audience. People can learn about the issue and the services that are available without needing to personally seek out information.

Finally, there is a strong possibility that there will be at least one audience member privately struggling with an abusive relationship who will have an emotional response to the presentation. A professional who has worked with victims and knows how to deal with their trauma will be able to calm them down and arrange for counseling and other support.

VICTIM SURVIVORS

Perhaps the most powerful thing an agency can do if it is directly involved in the workshop is to bring in an actual survivor to talk to participants. Having a victim tell what it is like to be beaten and traumatized by a partner and to describe how their job performance deteriorated will probably make the strongest impression and be the most memorable part of the training. It puts a face on the subject and can make even the most skeptical person in the audience at least consider the value of the program. Unfortunately, it is only too easy to find a woman who has lost a job because of their abuser (whether she was fired, demoted, or even assaulted at work). The local domestic violence service provider might know someone who is willing and capable of speaking to a group about their experience. However, if you are thinking of adding this element to a training program, remember that this person will feel very exposed and vulnerable standing up in front of a group of strangers to describe the horrors she endured, especially if it is her first time. It is the trainer's responsibility to make sure that the audience is respectful and empathetic.

Points for Consideration

STRONG REACTIONS

Family violence and its repercussions are not easy topics of discussion. Few people will be able to digest and contemplate all of its aspects without the subject touching some deep personal nerve. It is not an impersonal, technical topic and will probably elicit some controversy. Trainers should anticipate a range of reactions, from emphatic criticism to tearful, emotional response.

As we said, it is not uncommon to have in the training audience someone who has been abused at some time in their lives. If they share this information, it can be quite powerful. However, think carefully about content: Descriptions and details about physical and sexual abuse will spark immediate and very intense reaction. Extremely graphic or vivid audiovisual material will capture participants' attention, but it can also trigger painful memories. Domestic violence training programs for advocates, police, and court officials frequently include an audio presentation of what is referred to as the "*Lisa tape,"* provided by the New York City Victim Services Unit. It is an actual 911 call made by a young girl who is begging the police to come as her mother is assaulted. The abuser's yelling, the screams of the victim, and the cries of the child are so wrenching that anyone who hears it is deeply affected. Again, while material such as this establishes the severity of the issue and instills resolve in participants to learn how to support victims, it can further traumatize those who have heard such sounds in their own lives.

There might also be some personal revelations during the training session. The case studies, examples, and descriptions of what constitutes abuse might be enough to convince a participant that what she or he has been dealing with really is "domestic violence." The most experienced trainers and advocates know that this kind of realization can have an extremely devastating impact on an employee who makes this discovery in the presence of co-workers and supervisors. Intense feelings of vulnerability, fear, dread, and shame will rush through them as the material is presented, all while they are trying to maintain their professional and attentive appearance.

And it is not just the direct victims that will be vulnerable to such reactions. Adults who grew up in homes where abuse occurred have probably put the past behind them and created healthy relationships in their own lives, but listening to others discuss the topic has been known to evoke feelings and memories that were buried years and even decades ago.

Even men react strongly to the subject matter. In one program I conducted with a large group of construction managers and engineers, one burly, middle-aged man spoke out while I was talking. I was discussing the fact that victims frequently return to their abusers and explaining what the reasons for this are when he blurted out that *they deserve anything they get if they return.* Hoping to encourage dialogue on this topic, I asked this participant why he thought victims stay. However, he was getting visibly upset, so I said that although it is extremely difficult to understand the reasons, we don't need to understand in order to help. My instincts were that this was not someone who dismissed the whole issue of victimization, but rather that he was all too familiar with family violence and was speaking out of personal experience. Stating pressing time constraints, I offered to talk more on the subject after the workshop was over. Clearly, a topic as sensitive as this one requires us to carefully consider which materials we use, who the participants will be, and what possible reactions there will be to the content.

So how do you handle such reactions? A trainer must be aware of their audience at all times. An astute observer will detect distress and pain in a person's facial reactions or body language. Such individuals might excuse themselves to go to the restroom and not return for a lengthy period of time (or not at all). A person who has been hiding the abuse for years might not show any reaction. In others, the reaction will be only too obvious.

There are a couple of things you can do to prepare for these kinds of reactions. First, acknowledge at the beginning of the program that you know the topic is a difficult one to discuss and that some of the participants will have personal, firsthand knowledge of the subject. This implies that the issue is, unfortunately, common. People will understand that there is a possibility that one or more participants is a victim of abuse (or is close to someone who is) and that any visceral response will be normal.

The crucial part of the lesson, in this case, will be the referral information. The training will do more than provide skills or information: it will actually provide a service and support. The trainer can provide helpful information on the Employee Assistance Program (internal or external) and try to arrange for time-off for appointments, confidentiality, and where to go for specific help. Adult survivors who have experienced childhood family violence or who have survived an abusive relationship will find local agencies useful in dealing with long-term after-effects. (Note: It is not uncommon for a participant to ask for information or collect materials "for a friend" when it is really for themselves.)

One of the clearest benefits of having a domestic violence advocate present during the training is that they can better identify, know how to approach, and offer assistance to anyone who appears to be distressed by the training. Try to arrange for and then to stay after the training session to talk to participants privately, and be sure to announce this at the beginning.

USE OF HUMOR

Trainers use humor in their workshops to keep people engaged and interested and to make the whole program more enjoyable. Use jokes and humor to liven a presentation, but never take the issue of abuse lightly. You might be inclined to make glib comments to ease the tension or decrease the severity of the subject, but be aware that this detracts from the importance of the training and de-emphasizes the purpose of the whole program. Humor can be deeply insulting to those who know that it is no laughing matter.

MALE AUDIENCES

Domestic violence professionals judiciously use humor when there is disbelief or apathy about the topic, particularly where all the participants are men. Presenting statistics and case histories that show that most abusers are men to a room full of men might leave them with the impression that they are being blamed or labeled as abusers.

One way to deal with this is to make sure that you use gender-neutral terms to refer to victims and abusers. Acknowledge that there are situations when the man in the relationship is the legitimate victim. Do not get into a debate about whether or not there are more male victims than female victims or whether or not most husbands live in fear of their "old lady." The statistics will refute any of their arguments, but it is always a tricky situation when an argument develops between a trainer and participants.

It is sometimes best to avoid any "women vs. men" discussions. Simply explain how men play a vital role in victim support and in helping to end the violence. Most of the participants will have wives, sisters, and even daughters, and they have all had a mother. Showing how much victims need their support will strengthen their confidence in the program. Another thing you can do is to have a man present part of the session, such as a senior official or veteran employee who strongly supports and understands the issue (and who has the respect of the participants).

Do not let the possibility of negative reaction discourage an HR training team from delivering this program. There will be more positive than negative responses, especially when participants affirm what the trainer says about domestic abuse. If there is a strong sense of trust among employees, someone is likely to speak up about their own experience with devastating family violence, such as a supervisor, a family member, or a friend of a victim. Having a co-worker stand up and testify to the severity of the issue is often the strongest point of a training program. Be sensitive to the time constraints of the agenda, but by all means, make time for this person to describe their experience, and then thank them for having the courage to share it.

Low-Key Outreach

Training alone will not change a person's behavior or belief. This will require repeated and constant reminders of why everyone in the company should be concerned about domestic violence. Holding frequent training sessions is not practical and might even turn employees off. Try distributing "awareness" material once in a while to reaffirm the company's support. This will refresh the issue and keep the program going. A brief newsletter article can illustrate the company's efforts and initiatives, again conveying the message that it cares for its employees. Inserts placed in pay envelopes are another effective way to let every employee know about new regulations and programs. Pamphlets, brochures, flyers with tear-off information, and even small cards can be left in restrooms so victims get this much-needed information without fear of embarrassment.

There is a reason why low-key outreach is best: A victim's life is often completely controlled by their abuser. Their pockets and purses are probably searched regularly, and their every waking moment might be tracked. A victim is often severely punished if it is discovered that she has information on a domestic violence program. I was told about one woman who kept a small card with referral information in her shoe until she was able to hide it in the recesses of her closet. Though her clothing and pocketbook were regularly searched, her abuser did not find the card. Years later, this worn, old card was taken out of its hiding place and used when the woman had finally had enough of the abuse and was ready to seek help.

Information and awareness can also be brought out into the open to raise overall awareness. Posters illustrating the company's stance on the issue can be placed in break rooms or employee gathering places to create a supportive atmosphere and send a message that people condemn abusive behavior (resources for this material can be found in the Appendix). A cautionary note: If you choose to develop your own material, try not to use extremely graphic images of abused women or of violence, because this tends to make people turn away. The most effective message is one of support and understanding.

DISCUSSION GROUPS

Finally, nothing raises awareness as well as dialogue. Try having a brown bag or "lunch and learn" in formal discussion group before or after a program where only those interested attend. Offered during the lunch hour, the sessions can be facilitated by someone from HR and a representative from the local domestic violence agency. The purpose is simply to promote awareness. All you need is a large room. If space provides, participants can sit in a circle to encourage discussion. The format can be based on responses to a simple True or False questionnaire (provided in the Appendix) that the participants fill out at the beginning. Spend the rest of the session reviewing each question and going over the stereotypes and misconceptions that many people have regarding domestic violence. While there is value in declaring a general commitment to confidentiality about anything said in the meeting, facilitators must be careful not to let the gathering turn into a support group—it is simply a discussion to raise awareness.

Although individual disclosures can be a powerful component, we strongly advise you not to promote or encourage these personal accounts. They should be shared in an actual support-group setting. Having a representative from a local agency present to address personal issues and refer participants to services is the best way to go.

Conclusion

In this chapter, we outlined the approach organizations should take to developing a program on the subject of domestic violence in order to create a safer and more supportive workplace and help employee-victims. Managers and supervisors are critical in this effort, as are agencies and professional victim advocates. It is the organization as a whole, however, that must set the stage and the tone for an effective and meaningful intervention. Organization-wide training can help do that.

Chapter 11

Making a Difference

Earlier in the book, I related the story of an employee who was harassed and threatened at work. With the support of her company, she was able to free herself from the threat and persecution she endured from the abuser, and was later promoted for her excellent job performance. This woman eventually left the company to move back home. In 2003, she attended a conference on domestic violence in the workplace to present an award to her former employer. Here is an excerpt from that speech:

> Because I wanted to get away from him, he tried to get me terminated from my job, tried to force me into quitting, tried to have my children taken from me, tried to get me evicted. He tried to ruin my life and he was obsessed with that thought. Many times I thought there was no future for me.
>
> But I was wrong.
>
> You see, I had people that believed in me, and they believed so much in me, I had to believe in myself. My employer, my co-workers, and my friends. And, as time went on, I started getting that "eye of the tiger" that I used to have. I started feeling like **me** again. I began to see things in a different light—that if they believed in me so much, how could I not? If **they** saw me as a good employee and a good person, how could I ever feel different? I was a good mother. I was a good person. I was smart and capable. I was strong, and they gave that back to me, and I will never forget them for doing that for me.

You might ask, How did your employer benefit from this? It cost them money, time, and a lot of frustration.

My family thinks the world of Software Completions. My parents still have a daughter, my sisters have their sister, and my sons have their mother. And, more importantly, I have them. My life is fulfilled because Stan Dilley and my co-workers at Software Completions are such caring and wonderful people. Should an opportunity ever come up to send business their way, I will do it, because no one company deserves to be an overwhelming success like they do. Stan Dilley said something once that I will never forget. He said, "We do our very best to take care of our clients every way we can. How can we do any less for an employee?"

Would I even have that, if it were not for Software Completions? I don't think so. I could never have done it alone. Sometimes, you have to ask for help, and I thank God that there are people in this world like them so I could ask for help. I never in a million years dreamed that it would be such a long and tiring road, but if they complained at all, it wasn't to me.

This experience has made me think of many things. How can someone be dedicated to a job, and not family? How does one have sincere dedication to one thing and not another? Perhaps true dedication is in the heart, where the drive and desire to succeed in a business is every bit as strong as that to the family or to principles by which they live.

> Colleen Gorski, speaking at the October 30, 2003
> *"Don't Let Domestic Violence Hurt Your Business"* Summit
> in Chapel Hill, North Carolina

If the simple value of these principles is not evident enough, this final chapter will look at the economic benefits of addressing the issue of domestic violence in the workplace. We will explore the impact by those companies that understand the prevalence and severity of abuse on their communities—not only because they can open their checkbooks, but because they can reduce the frequency and impact of domestic violence in the communities they serve and are sustained by.

The Benefits to Developing a Program

If all the measures and considerations detailed in the book appear impractical or there is resistance from management to be proactive, the short- and long-term benefits outlined here should help your argument. From developing policy and training staff members to helping an individual employee who has nowhere else to turn, a company that commits to addressing this social illness will be improving the productivity of its employees and will thus gain the respect of the activists and investors. Domestic violence awareness is indeed a business issue.

SAFETY

A formal program increases awareness and preparedness for any threats of violence. As illustrated in the earlier chapters, one of the greatest and most common risks to a company comes from the domestic partners of employees. What goes on in these relationships, even if they work for the same employer, remains a mystery to most employers. By creating an atmosphere where employees feel comfortable disclosing information about volatile (and embarrassing) situations, management will have an earlier warning of threat. An established threat assessment team using guidelines already developed will be vital components to an effective response. If the employer provides adequate resources and time to assess the risk and develop a security plan, the threat has less of a chance of becoming a headline story.

INCREASED PRODUCTIVITY

Victims will inevitably have problems at work, whether it is due to the lingering effects of the abuse at home or abuser harassment while on the job. When a victim employee is supported by her company, she stands a better chance of leaving the abusive situation and establishing a stable and healthy home life. She will have less need for sick leave and health benefits and won't be as tardy or absent as she was and will be more productive in her job. These are all objective, quantifiable improvements that show the value of having a domestic violence program. Time and again, it has been shown that an employee who has been supported by her employer will later show up for work on time, concentrate better, and have the confidence to excel. The victim survivors who speak out at outreach awareness events almost always express their amazement and joy in the new levels of self-reliance and ambition they now feel. An astute supervisor will be able to see the potential. Given the opportunity to handle their personal crisis, victims quickly return to higher levels of performance, to the astonishment of everyone involved.

We have said throughout the book that the employee-victim who is given time and understanding support returns the favor by becoming even more loyal to their company. Work environment, co-worker relations, and fair treatment are just some factors that contribute to every employee's decision to remain with their company. When owners and managers demonstrate care and concern, all employees will judge how it was handled. The value of having a workforce that truly respects the leaders of a company and wants to help it succeed cannot be understated.

PUBLIC RELATIONS

This same high regard can extend into the community where the company does its business. In a world where clients choose services and products based on a corporation's reputation and behavior, taking a socially responsible stance can have a direct and positive effect on profits.

Women make up the largest percentage of overall consumers, and they will choose to support companies that treat their people well and act as responsible members of the larger community—not only in industries that are specifically tailored to women (such as cosmetics), but in virtually every type of business. There clearly are economic benefits to presenting a positive and progressive image of social responsibility.

No company wants negative publicity, but that is what will result if an organization fires an employee because their personal situation poses a risk or inconvenience and a lawsuit is filed. While the risk of losing the court case is arguably low, the impact of any negative press coverage is likely to be far greater than any savings (as many companies can testify). Conversely, a proactive and progressive approach wins the admiration of not only the victim, but also the local advocates and community leaders who have frequent contact with the media and legislators. Developing and implementing a domestic violence program and supporting employee-victims will cast a favorable light on a company's reputation. Often, a company establishes its civil responsibility through foundation-giving or community relations programs—these efforts are certainly needed and appreciated—but a business that internalizes its philanthropic efforts by protecting and respecting its own employees is making a very real commitment that will be publicly lauded. A company that refuses to tolerate abusive behavior sends a clear message that such actions will have consequences. Many advocacy organizations and victim rights groups will gladly advertise and promote the good work of your company through newsletters, public awareness events, and direct communication with their substantial membership.

The benchmark study commissioned by Liz Claiborne, Inc., conducted by Patrice Tanaka and Company in 2002, asked senior executives of Fortune 1000 companies just whose responsibility it is to combat domestic violence. Most of the responding executives said that responsibility should be with a governmental agency, law enforcement, or the courts. Only 12 percent of respondents believed that employers have an opportunity to be leaders for change. However, few can argue that in today's world, corporations play a significant role in the culture and social environment where they hire, advertise, produce, and sell their products or services.

There are advantages to creating a more productive and safer workplace and there are public relations benefits, but reducing domestic violence throughout the community has a long-term and lasting impact. Domestic violence has been widely recognized as a major contributor to other social illnesses, such as crime, drug abuse, and economic poverty. Popular and well-funded programs dedicated to supporting victims and stopping abusive behaviors have a deep impact on the entire population. A city or town that has good services to help battered women will have a healthier pool of job applicants and a more financially successful customer base that will be selective in which businesses they support. Perhaps most importantly, more children will grow up never knowing the distress and chaos of a violent home.

Social Responsibility

So what can an organization or business do to address the issue of domestic violence on a community level? We have addressed policy development guidelines for training employees, and procedures for intervention. Now let's look at several easy but powerful things that a company can do immediately if it wants to be part of the solution.

WORKING WITH SHELTERS

A clear place to start is by supporting local agencies that work with victims of domestic violence. These organizations are professionally run and staffed, but many scrape by just to keep their services running. Domestic violence shelters and agencies do not charge a victim for their services, so it is vital that they can obtain support through other means. The most direct way you can support such agencies is through corporate financial contributions. Almost all of them are non-profit organizations, so your gift is probably tax-deductible (making donations all that more attractive and compelling). Employees can share in the effort through the annual United Way fund-raising campaign if the organization running the shelter is approved for United Way money. (However, during the campaign period, no single agency can be suggested or singled out.) Non-profit organizations often rely on government grants to remain operational, but in many cases, the agency has to come up with matching funds in order to get the grant award. The business community can provide this important funding.

PROVIDE IN-KIND SUPPORT

Corporate support does not always have to come in the form of a check: in-kind support often fulfills part of the matching funds requirement. These organizations might need services or products that can be readily supplied by a business at no cost. Donations of used furniture, office equipment, computers, and supplies are often dearly needed by such organizations. As systems are upgraded or offices are refurbished, consider donating what you no longer need to the advocacy agency. They may be able to trade what they can't use with a sister agency, or sell the items to raise revenue.

Company services are another excellent source of support. Internal resources such as information technology, consulting, or accounting can greatly benefit a shelter or community agency. It is this kind of business expertise that makes an agency more effective and productive to the community. A frequent and simple way to help is to use your in-house printing capability to help the agency produce brochures, training manuals, and fact sheets. All in-kind donations are likely to be tax-deductible, thus reducing a company's tax liability. In order to learn how you can help, ask the agencies what they need and don't have.

JOIN THE BOARD OR A COMMITTEE

Perhaps the greatest help that you personally can provide is to give your time. Most domestic violence service providers are non-profits: Their boards need members who have organizational skills and community connections. Successful leaders are needed to mentor and teach an agency how to excel. While the commitment level may vary, most boards simply require members to attend a monthly meeting, with interspersed contact made through various committees and projects. Talk with the director or board chairperson to learn more about the opportunities and level of involvement. The rewards will far outweigh the time expenditure: The contacts made through board involvement, the integration into the community, and most importantly, the personal involvement in the agency's mission have made lasting impressions on many business leaders.

SPONSOR EVENTS

One clear means of collaboration is to host an awareness event produced by the advocacy agency. For example, you can host a workshop on domestic violence in the workplace that is open to the entire business community. This might be a pioneering opportunity. Your organization can talk about how it has implemented its policies on domestic violence as well as trained its own employees. Acting as a role model for other companies is good public relations. Shelters and agencies often promote a variety of events to increase awareness. They go into the schools and to fairs, hold exhibitions displaying the therapeutic artwork of victims and their children, and hold vigils in memory of murdered victims. A company can sponsor, advertise, provide refreshments, and even host such events at their facility. Developing such partnerships is the key to the success of any venture.

COORDINATE YOUR EFFORTS WITH THOSE OF OTHER BUSINESSES

One successful business collaboration took place in the tourist town of Asheville, North Carolina. Businesses that serve the public directly, such as retail shops and restaurants, collaborated with Interlace, a long-term residential program for battered women in an event called "Shop for Change," which promoted awareness and generated revenue (a portion of all sales and proceeds went to support the agency's budget). An aggressive campaign announced the date and listed participating businesses through the use of posters, public service announcements, and media relations. Everyone involved benefited from this successful event: The housing program received the funds to help more victims start their lives over, free from abuse. Likewise, businesses were recognized for their social responsibility in giving back to the community. Socially conscious citizens purposely came out to spend money and support the effort; a majority of customers said they went into stores or restaurants they had never been into before, just because of the sign on their door proclaiming their participation in the movement. Whatever portion of sales that was donated to the cause (which were also tax-deductible) was clearly offset by the general increase in overall buying that day. Finally, there was a long-term gain: a new sense of "community" and collaboration among businesses. The event helped establish business-to-business relationships that had a broader, beneficial effect on the market.

Working with Other Organizations

These local community events have been magnified on a state and even national level through public-private partnerships. Contact information for many of these programs is available in the Appendix.

Many global corporations have recognized the workplace need to raise awareness and take safety precautions. They also know how they can make a difference in the world that buys their products or services. Companies such as Liz Claiborne, American Express, Altria, and Polaroid have been pioneers in addressing this issue internally and making an impact through support of victim advocacy agencies and promotion of awareness efforts. But even smaller companies can become involved with the movement by joining one of the many dynamic associations committed to doing something about domestic violence.

The Family Violence Prevention Fund has joined with employers and unions to form the National Workplace Resource Center on Domestic Violence. It also started the "Work to End Domestic Violence" Day, held nationally every October. Reaching out from its base in San Francisco, the fund has recruited the support of U.S. companies to lead their communities in addressing domestic violence in the workplace.

The Corporate Alliance to End Partner Violence, based in Chicago, has members across the nation who work to eliminate family violence. Since 1995, this Alliance has collaborated to develop model materials and promote awareness events, using its substantial resources to instigate change. Membership benefits include extensive support in policy development, staff training, development of survey instruments, networking opportunities, and access to nationally acclaimed presenters.

The Massachusetts pioneer alliance Employers Against Domestic Violence (EADV) provides tools, resources, and expertise to help organizations develop policy and train personnel. It is also creating a base of socially responsible companies to network, share ideas, and generate overall awareness of the issue. Started in 1996 by the law firm of Mintz, Levin, Cohn, Ferris, Glovsky, and Popeo, PC, the association has had an undeniable impact, not only in New England, but across the country. It is this organization that developed the landmark study of over 90 employers from a wide range of industries mentioned earlier that assessed how a batterer's behavior directly affects the workplace.

A more recent alliance is the Safe@Work coalition, which brings together private employers, domestic violence advocacy organizations, government entities, and labor unions to provide outreach and awareness to the global community, as well as resources and tools to help any size company combat the issue. Their Web site is a tremendous resource.

Attorneys in Colorado came together to create awareness and provide the means to implement change. The Colorado Bar Association has hosted successful state-wide summits and regional programs to spread the word. Their Web site is an excellent source for information, model programs, and action steps.

The Department of Justice of Louisiana has also stepped forward. It provides direct training in regional and onsite locations; participants are encouraged to sign a pledge declaring their commitment to protect and support victims in their workplace through policy and programs.

Finally, Peace@Work has its own program, known as Employers for Violence Prevention. This association takes a stand against all forms and sources of violence in the workplace, but its primary focus is on protecting victims of abuse and holding perpetrator-employees accountable for their actions. While membership does provide the benefits of additional resources and support, the value of the public proclamation to strive toward creating a violence-free workplace has tremendous significance to employees and customers.

Numerous other programs are springing up around the country, testifying to the increased awareness and severity of the issue. Membership and participation in any of these organizations is free or at a nominal cost. However, the benefits of belonging to an association with such august corporate membership and the opportunity to share resources can have far-reaching impacts on an organization's reputation and public standing.

Appendix

Discussion Points:
Myths About Domestic Violence

Note for Facilitator: Use the following true-false statements to generate a group discussion about the subject of domestic violence.

1. **Victims can leave the abuse anytime they want.**

   ❑ True   ❑ False

   While every victim wants the abuse to end, she/he often does not want the relationship to end. She/he is aware that substantial obstacles will have to be overcome and that the family might be in grave danger if they leave.

   Among the challenges to leaving are these:

   ▲ She/he still loves the abuser.
   ▲ She/he does not have the money, job skills, or support to be able to live alone.
   ▲ She/he does not feel capable or smart enough to survive without the abuser.
   ▲ She/he has nowhere to go.
   ▲ Family, friends, and the community tell her/him to stay and "work it through."
   ▲ The abuser has threatened to kill her/him if she/he leaves.

2. **Domestic violence only occurs in poor communities, to uneducated people at the lower end of the socio-economic scale.**

   ❑ True   ❑ False

   Studies and court statistics show that domestic abuse occurs to a wide range of individuals, regardless of income, educational level, age, race, sexual orientation, or religion. Many abusers are highly paid, influential, and powerful figures such as judges, preachers, doctors, and attorneys. Domestic violence does not stem from lack of money, education, resources, or good upbringing, but from the abuser's need to control the victim at all costs. Many successful individuals obtained their status through manipulation and assertive behavior. They use these same tools in their abusive personal relationships.

3. **Domestic violence is just an angry outburst or lover's spat, when emotions get out of control.**

   ❑ True   ❑ False

   Abusers often are not hostile or aggressive to anyone else but their victim. They can control their anger whenever they choose. Domestic violence covers criticism, sexual abuse, economic control, emotional degradation, and efforts to control and isolate the victim, all of which can be perpetrated in a calm and sedate manner. Domestic violence is a pattern of behaviors. Rage is just one of the tools used to control and intimidate the victim. It is often planned and contrived to keep the victim down.

4. **It would have never have happened if the abuser had not been drunk (or high, or otherwise under the influence).**

   ❑ True   ❑ False

   Substance abuse is too often used as an excuse for battering. It does influence and affect a person's behavior, but it does not create new impulse or thoughts. It often just lowers the inhibition to carry out feelings already there. It does not excuse the crime any more than a drunk driver who kills a victim should be excused just because they were inebriated. If an abuser struck the victim the last time he was drunk, he knows what might happen if he starts drinking again.

The substance abuse and the domestic abuse must each be addressed, but taking care of one issue will not solve the other.

5. **Domestic violence is not very common.**

   ❑ True   ❑ False

   Studies indicate that one-third to one-fifth of women surveyed state that they have been physically assaulted by an intimate partner at some point in their lives. Despite a woman's fear of strangers in dark parking lots or burglars, she is more likely to be killed by a current or former partner, according to many states' statistics. Domestic violence is often the leading cause of injury for women—it is more common than car accidents, falls, or other assaults.

   Research is not the only way to find the truth. Most people personally know of a case or situation in which someone lives in fear of their domestic partner.

6. **Women abuse just as often as men do. They are just as violent, if not more so.**

   ❑ True   ❑ False

   While there are some isolated, smaller studies suggesting this, the majority of larger, more-comprehensive studies show that it is men who are doing most of the abusing. In terms of injury, the women are suffering the abuse. The clearest indication is that far more women are killed by their partners than are men. However, there are cases where men are legitimate victims of abuse.

7. **The victim often antagonizes the abuser or starts the fight.**

    ❏ True   ❏ False

    It is very difficult to design or conduct research on who "started the fight" or how "difficult" the victim is. One cause of abuse is when the victim has been having an affair. Whatever reason the abuser chooses for his or her behavior, the simple answer is that there is no excuse for assaulting a partner. Victims very often do all they can to appease the abuser and prevent a hostile reaction or another assault for the smallest mistake.

8. **Domestic violence is an inter-relational dynamic. It takes two to fight, and both parties need to change to make it stop.**

    ❏ True   ❏ False

    The decision to abuse and assault is always the abuser's choice to make. It is up to the individual to control their behavior, no matter what. The notion that both parties are responsible turns the problem into a marital or relationship issue, which suggests that the victim is partially responsible for being assaulted. This view often shifts the focus, putting the blame on the victim instead of the person who commits the criminal act.

9. **What looks like abuse is just the customary behavior of that culture. Some men need to be "macho" and want women to be subservient.**

    ❏ True   ❏ False

    Despite culture and custom, it is never acceptable for anyone to be abused or threatened. Stating that this is the way men and women are in certain cultural or ethnic groups is only making an excuse for the abuser. There is no need to control or abuse another person in any relationship. Physical assaults and threats are a crime, no matter what the context.

10. There is no point in helping a victim leave, since she/he will just go back to the abuser in the end.

❏ True ❏ False

While it is often frustrating when a victim lacks the resources or the confidence or is otherwise convinced to return to the abuser, leaving an abusive relationship is not an event. It is a process that can involve several attempts before a victim is able to leave for good.

Each time she does leave, she learns a little more about the process and about new services that can help the next time. If she does not find the support she needs, it is less likely that she will attempt to leave again.

11. Abusers are crazy sociopaths who usually have criminal records and a history of violent behavior.

❏ True ❏ False

Just as victims come from a wide range of backgrounds, so do the abusers. It is not uncommon for an abuser to be someone with very high standing in the community, holding a graduate degree and an important position. Similarly, an abuser might be known as a "really nice guy" or just your average Joe. Again and again, after a horrible homicide-suicide, there is great disbelief and shock that something so violent has happened to this couple.

Support Steps: Checklist

SUPPORT STEPS

▲ Allow for time off to make legal, medical, and advocacy appointments and meet other obligations.

Options to consider are:
- ❑ Flex scheduling
- ❑ Sick leave
- ❑ Shared time
- ❑ Compensatory time
- ❑ Vacation leave
- ❑ Leave without pay

▲ Change personnel information immediately.

- ❑ Personal contact information (maintain strict confidentiality)
- ❑ Paycheck deposit allocation
- ❑ Beneficiary information for:
  - Health benefits
  - Retirement accounts (including 401-K and pension funds)
  - Life insurance

▲ Use leniency and understanding in any performance evaluations

▲ Assist in the transfer of the victim to a new division or plant, if available and desired

▲ Provide referrals to support systems, including the following:

- ❑ Employee Assistance Program
- ❑ Domestic Violence advocacy services
- ❑ Legal aid offices
- ❑ Law enforcement agencies
- ❑ Social services

Security Measures: Checklist

ASSESSING THE THREAT AND IMPLEMENTING SECURITY

The following list of security measures contains suggestions and ideas, not specific steps for every situation. Each individual situation requires a comprehensive assessment by appropriate personnel (such as human resources, security, and law enforcement) to determine the best course of action. This guideline serves only to provide a range of optional actions that management can take to protect the victim and the workplace.

Response plan if perpetrator approaches the workplace:

❑ Call law enforcement!
❑ If there is no direct threat or court order against the individual, notify security if available.
❑ Lock all entrances to the facility.
❑ Warn the targeted victim(s).
❑ Notify all personnel, especially management and individuals planning security.
❑ Allow passage on an escape route or to a safe location that has been pre-designated.

Develop a plan to secure the workplace and protect employees:

❑ Distribute information regarding the description of the perpetrator and their vehicle to security and front desk personnel.
❑ Request increased police patrols.
❑ Obtain copy of restraining order for security and/or management, if available.
❑ Limit access to building; use only one entrance.
❑ Provide buzzer alarms and/or panic buttons.
❑ Increase security measures: fencing, additional lighting, and cameras.

Target hardening of the victim:

❏ Change victim's assigned parking space/area to the safest location.
❏ Escort the victim to and from her/his car each day.
❏ Reassign the victim to a different shift or workspace, or to safer conditions and duties.
❏ Provide emergency cell phones (available from most Domestic Violence shelters).
❏ Screen victim's incoming calls and/or provide a new extension and e-mail address.
❏ Create a code word to use in emergencies.
❏ Maintain previous phone or e-mail extensions in order to record abuser's messages for evidence.
❏ Provide support for victim's security at their home or make other safety arrangements.

Most-effective measures if threat is deemed imminent and lethal:

❏ Hire off-duty law enforcement officers as security.
❏ Request that a squad car be parked in front of facility.
❏ Lock all entrances to facility, allowing passage only to valid visitors.
❏ Ensure easy egress for safe evacuation.
❏ Remove victim from family.
❏ Assign victim to work at other location, or allow time off.
❏ Hire security consultant, who can:
  • Provide extensive, customized, and expert advice on security measures.
  • Have an investigator to track the perpetrator's movements.

Organizational Resources

National Hotline and Referral Service
24-hour national hotline to locate local domestic violence
shelters and services to help victims of abuse.
1(800)799-SAFE (7233)

Peace@Work
A non-profit organization dedicated to violence prevention in
the workplace. The director of the agency is the author of this
book.
www.peaceatwork.org

Legal Momentum
Excellent resource for employment law issues, civil suits, and
legislation around the country. Also provides Employment
Rights for Survivors of Abuse (ERSA), a source for legal advice,
public education, and technical assistance.
www.legalmomentum.org

Corporate Alliance to End Partner Violence
An association of employers who have taken a stand against
partner violence. Membership speaking opportunities, and
resources are available.
www.caepv.org

Family Violence Prevention Fund
Pioneer agency developing outreach and awareness on domestic
violence in the workplace. Runs the Workplace Resource Center,
which makes resources and statistics available.
www.endabuse.org

Colorado Bar Association
Resources for employers in Colorado and across the country.
Excellent Action Plan documents available for developing a
program immediately.
www.makeityourbusiness.org

Safe@Work Coalition

Coalition of private and public employers committed to increasing awareness and developing resources for employers to all types and sizes. Extensive and comprehensive Web site available for human resources professionals, labor union activists, and business owners.

www.safeatworkcoalition.org

A Model Policy

Domestic Abuse and Company Responsibility

Purpose: As domestic violence is a serious threat to the safety and security of our workforce, (Company) is dedicated to increasing awareness of this issue, offering support to victims of abuse, and holding perpetrators accountable for their actions. It is the intention of this policy to promote a healthy, safe environment where all employees are encouraged to report any concerns, seek assistance when necessary, and help foster a respectful and understanding environment.

This policy does not obligate (Company) to address any reports or allegations in any particular manner.

Scope: This policy applies to any persons hired by (Company), including employees, temporary support, vendors, and/or contracted individuals. The other party in the abusive relationship, whether victim or abuser, does not have to have any relationship with (Company) for the policy to apply.

Definitions: *Domestic Violence:* A pattern of behavior meant to threaten, harass, and coerce the victim in order to establish and maintain control and dominance. Along with physical trauma, it can include emotional, psychological, sexual, and financial abuse devised to exert control. Domestic violence can occur between current or former relationships, and between heterosexual or same-sex couples, either married, living together, or living separately.

Domestic violence can include but is not limited to:

- ▲ Physical violence
- ▲ Sexual assault or rape
- ▲ Threats
- ▲ Intimidation
- ▲ Harassment by any communication means
- ▲ Stalking
- ▲ Damage to property

Victim or Survivor: The victim is the person who is the target of the abuse. This can be an individual who is still in the relationship or is trying to leave or has left the abuser. While the vast majority of victims are women, men can be victims of abuse as well, and will be entitled to the same consideration in developing support and protections. Domestic violence can happen to anyone, with no distinction made regarding race, age, culture, ethnicity, religion, sexual orientation, or economic or educational status.

Abuser, Batterer, Perpetrator: The person who commits acts of domestic violence against the victim or survivor.

Domestic Violence Service Provider: A community agency that offers services to victims of abuse, which can include a temporary safe house or shelter, counseling, support groups, or court accompaniment. Other community resources include law enforcement, legal assistance, social services, and health care institutions.

Prevention and Awareness:

(Company) will provide training opportunities for staff to increase awareness of the issue of domestic violence, demonstrate how to respond to potential cases, explain what (Company) can do to offer assistance, and describe what community resources are available.

Dissemination of this policy will be initially made to all employees through company memos, staff meetings, and formal training programs. New employees will be introduced to the policy during the orientation process.

Prohibited Actions and Sanctions:

Acts of domestic violence perpetrated by employees within the workplace will not be tolerated, and violators will face disciplinary actions up to and including dismissal.

The prohibited actions include any employee using company resources, equipment, communications devices, or vehicles to commit acts of domestic violence, or any employee who engages in such behavior while conducting company business, regardless of the location.

It may be determined that an employee's off-duty conduct constitutes grounds for disciplinary actions up to and including dismissal, depending on the nature of the offense and its potential impact on the company, and the employee's ability to fulfill their duties. A judgment in a court of law can provide the evidence to substantiate allegations of any domestic violence acts.

Successful completion of a treatment program for batterers and/or participation with the Employee Assistance Program may be a requirement for job retention.

**Support
and
Protections:**

An employee will not be disciplined or discriminated against solely on the basis of his or her role as a victim of domestic violence.

It is (Company's) position to recognize the victim's right to self-determination. The victim will be allowed to direct the course of action that affects their life, with no pressure or coercion from management. The (Company's) primary goal is the safety of the employee and the workplace. As such, it will not require a victim to leave the abuser, although this action will be supported as much as is reasonably possible.

When an employee has been identified as a victim of abuse, either through self-disclosure or through an employee meeting, a supervisor or human resources staff person can refer the individual to an Employee Assistance Program and/or to a domestic violence agency. Pamphlets and contact information for such programs will be made available to all employees.

The Employee Assistance Program can be reached at (xxx) xxx-xxxx. The local domestic violence service provider is (NAME) and their contact number is (xxx) xxx-xxxx. The statewide coalition number is (xxx) xxx-xxxx. The national 24-hour, toll-free referral number is (800) 799-SAFE.

As victims will need time off for counseling and legal and medical appointments, management will work with the victim to arrange their schedule. Options to consider are:

▲ Flexible scheduling
▲ Sick leave

▲ Shared time
▲ Compensatory time
▲ Vacation leave
▲ Leave without pay

Management is mindful that certain domestic problems might require extended periods of time to resolve and may consider options to allow for longer absences.

Additional support for the victim can be offered by expediting any change in information regarding benefits or beneficiary. This includes but is not limited to paycheck deposits, retirement benefits, health insurance coverage, and contact information.

While management reserves the right to address any work production issues, the impact of domestic violence in performance evaluations will be considered. (Company) realizes that surviving, terminating, and recovering from an abusive relationship is a lengthy and difficult process.

Once a threat to the workplace has been identified, management may take action to assess the risk and implement measures to reduce the likelihood of violence committed against the victim, co-workers, or the workplace as a whole.

Safety of all employees is the primary goal of (Company) and will be the basis of any management decisions regarding the case.

Any and all actions taken will be at the sole discretion of company management; the company is not obligated to offer specific supportive actions for any particular employee.

Specific Roles and Responsibilities:

Employees: All employees will attend and participate in the domestic violence training provided by the human resource department.

All employees are prohibited from committing any act of domestic violence and/or using company resources to commit such acts, either at the workplace or while conducting company business. Perpetrators are strongly encouraged to contact the Employee Assistance Program and/or encouraged to participate in a batterer's treatment program.

Employees who are victims of domestic violence are encouraged to disclose this to a staff member in the human resources department or to a department supervisor if the abuser poses a threat to the workplace. These employees are also encouraged to contact the Employee Assistance Program and/or the local domestic violence service provider if job performance is impacted or they need support.

If any employee believes that there is a threat to the workplace, whether they witness a concern or are personally involved, the employee shall notify a supervisor or human resources staff member as soon as possible. In the event of imminent violence, employees should notify police immediately, and then notify a supervisor.

Supervisors: All supervisors must attend and participate in the domestic violence training provided by the Human Resources department.

Supervisors should make certain that all employees are aware of and have access to the domestic violence policy.

If an employee discloses that she or he is a victim of abuse, the individual shall be referred to the Employee Assistance Program and/or the local domestic violence service provider. If a supervisor is made aware of any threat to the workplace, she or he shall notify Human Resources immediately. Their participation in threat assessment and implementation of security measures is vital to the safety of the workplace.

Human Resources: The Human Resources department shall provide training programs appropriate to the level of responsibility for every employee.

This department shall develop and maintain an implementation plan for the effective management of a specific and actual domestic violence case.

Human Resources shall be able to offer the appropriate materials and have contact information for any community resource that is able to assist victims of domestic abuse.

Any changes to benefits, such as arrangements regarding paycheck deposits, health insurance coverage, or retirement accounts can be offered and expedited to reflect changes in the employee's personal situation and residence.

Personnel contact information such as home address or temporary residence and phone numbers will be closely protected to ensure confidentiality and to prevent the abuser from discovering the victim's temporary or new residence or other information.

Security: Security personnel must attend and participate in the domestic violence training provided by the Human Resources department.

If it has been determined that there is indeed a threat to the workplace, Security's participation in any threat assessment and in the implementation of security measures is required to help reduce the occurrence and severity of any violence.

**Confiden-
tiality and
Non-
Retaliation
Clause:**

Management will try to protect the confidentiality of all reports and any information regarding an employee's involvement in a domestic violence situation. All communication about the case will be on a need-to-know basis. Any employee who makes a report in good faith regarding a domestic violence issue in the workplace shall not suffer any retaliation.

References

Ahrens, C., A. Blickenstaff, and S. Riger. (2000). Measuring interference with employment and education, reported by women with abusive partners. Preliminary data. *Violence and Victims:* 15(2): 161–172.

Collins, K., C. Schoen, S. Joseph, L. Duchon, E. Simantov, and M. Yellowitz. (May, 1999). Health Concerns across a Woman's Lifespan: The Commonwealth Fund 1998 Survey of Women's Health.

Couper, S. and L. Friedman. (1987). The cost of domestic violence: A preliminary investigation of the financial cost of domestic violence. In Violence on the Job: Identifying Risks and Developing Solutions, by Friedman, L., S. B. Tucker, P. R. Neville, and M. Imperial.

Gilmer, T. P., L. E. Saltzman, C. L. Wiszner, and T. M. Zink. (1999). Intimate partner violence against women: Do victims cost health plans more? *The Journal of Family Practice.* 48(6): 439–443.

Gist, J., A. Malecha, J. McFarlane, P. Schulz, et al. (2000). Indicators of intimate partner violence in women's employment: Implications for workplace action. *AAOHN Journal,* 48(5): 215.

LaRose v. State Mutual Life Assurance Co., No. 9322684 (215th District Court of Harris County, Texas. December 5, 1994).

Morracco, Beth (2000). Killed on the Clock. *American Journal of Industrial Medicine.* 37: 629–636.

Patrice Tanaka and Company, Inc. (October 16, 2002). "Corporate Leaders See Domestic Violence as a Major Problem That Affects Their Employees, According to Benchmark Survey by Liz Claiborne, Inc."

The Body Shop. (September, 1997). *The Many Faces of Domestic Violence and Its Impact on the Workplace.* New York: EDK Associates.

U.S. Bureau of Justice Statistics. (February, 2003). Crime Data Brief: Intimate Partner Violence, 1993–2001.

U.S. Department of Health and Human Services, National Center for Injury Prevention and Control. (March, 2003). *Costs of Intimate Partner Violence Against Women in the United States.* Atlanta: Centers for Disease Control and Prevention.

U.S. Department of Justice, National Institute of Justice. (November, 2000). *Full Report of the Prevalence, Incidence, and Consequences of Violence Against Women.* NCJ 183781, pp. 4, 13.

U.S. Department of Labor, Bureau of Labor Statistics. (2000). Census of Fatal Occupational Injuries: Table A-6 "Fatal occupational injuries by worker characteristics and event or exposure."

U.S. General Accounting Office. (November, 1998). Domestic Violence: Prevalence and Implications for Employment Among Welfare Recipients. 19 (GAO report to Congressional Committees).

Urban, B. Y. (2000). Anonymous Foundation Domestic Abuse Prevention Program Evaluation: Final Client Survey Report. Chicago: The University of Illinois.

Urban, B. Y., L. Bennett, and K. Schneider. (July, 1999). The University of Chicago: Illinois. Unpublished research report. Domestic Abuse Presentation Program Evaluation: Plant Survey Comparison Report.

G. R. VandenBos and R. Q. Bulatao, eds. (1996). Washington, D.C.: American Psychological Association: 154–155.

Wiscombe, Janet. (October 2002). *Workforce.*

Zachary, Mary-Kathryn. Precautionary Measures Curb Workplace Violence Liability. (September 1, 1998). *Supervision.*

About the Author

Johnny Lee is the founding director of Peace@Work, a non-profit organization committed to the prevention of violence in the workplace. He provides consulting services to businesses and non-profit organizations on the escalating problem of domestic violence, specializing in program development and training for human resource professionals, chambers of commerce, state and county agencies, and private corporations.

Before founding Peace@Work, Johnny Lee served as the workplace violence specialist for the North Carolina Office of State Personnel, where he was responsible for helping state agencies develop or revise their workplace violence policies to include a domestic violence component. He was an active member of the North Carolina Domestic Violence Commission, and has worked directly with victims of domestic violence from incident to prosecution as victim services coordinator for a major metropolitan police department. Before becoming involved with violence prevention, he spent six years heading up adventure and leadership programs for Outward Bound.

Johnny Lee sits on the boards of the North Carolina Continuity Business Planners, the North Carolina Interagency Council of Victim Services, and the North Carolina Victim Assistance Network, and participates in task forces to raise awareness and coordinate services to victims of family violence. He holds a Master's degree from Mankato State University in Minnesota and writes about issues related to the subject of domestic violence for such publications as *The*

Journal of Safe Management of Disruptive and Assaultive Behavior.

He can be contacted at: Peace@Work
4030 Wake Forest Road, Suite 300
Raleigh, NC 27609
(919) 274-5515
www.peaceatwork.org
jlee@peaceatwork.org